Read, MARK, Learn

Alexander Roper Vidler was born at Rye, Sussex, in 1899, and educated at Sutton Valence School, Selwyn College, Cambridge, and Wells Theological College. He was ordained in 1922 and worked in slum parishes in Newcastle-upon-Tyne and Birmingham, where he was involved in a famous dispute with Bishop Barnes.

During the 1939–45 war he was Warden of St Deiniol's Library, Hawarden, formerly the library of the great Mr Gladstone, and then became a Canon of St George's, Windsor, where he trained many middle-aged ordinands known as his Doves. He was a Fellow and Dean of King's College, Cambridge, 1956–67, becoming an Honorary Fellow in 1972.

Upon his formal retirement Dr Vidler became Mayor of Rye, a position he held for two terms – the fourth generation Vidler to do so.

He was also Editor of *Theology* 1939–64, and is the author of twenty-six books, including *Paul, Envoy Extraordinary* (with Malcolm Muggeridge, his close friend) and *Scenes From A Clerical Life*, both published by Collins.

ALEC R. VIDLER

Read, MARK, Learn

Collins
FOUNT PAPERBACKS

First published in Great Britain in 1980
by Fount Paperbacks

© Alec R. Vidler 1980

Made and printed in Great Britain by
William Collins Sons & Co Ltd, Glasgow

Contents

Preface

For many years now it has been my practice to study the Bible with groups of a dozen or fifteen people who have met regularly in order to learn more about the Christian faith and, by questioning and discussion, to help one another to see what the scriptures have to say to us today. It has fallen to me to introduce our sessions with comments on the book in the Bible that we were studying at the time. I have based my comments on the text of *The Common Bible* (or the Revised Standard Version), but members of the group have been encouraged to use other versions as well and to call attention to any striking differences in the translations. It has been suggested that my comments may be of use to other groups of people who meet to study the Bible, and also perhaps to individuals, and even to preachers. I should certainly like to hear more *expository* sermons and to see congregations attending church or chapel with their Bibles in their hands, prepared to follow an exposition of scripture. Hence my presumption in adding to the already large range of books in this field.

I have not sought to be original and am indebted to many other commentators more learned than myself. All my life, when studying the Bible, I have made notes on the text, notes culled from many sources, but not with any idea that I might one day want to publish them. I have also over the years collected a large number of biblical commentaries by authors of differing nationality, ecclesiastical allegiance, and theological stance.

I have naturally drawn on these notes and used these commentaries when preparing my own expositions. I will acknowledge my debts whenever I can, but if from time to time I have unwittingly plagiarized the work of others without acknowledgement I hope I may be forgiven. The books I have found most useful are specified in the list of abbreviations on p. 173.

My comments are based on a grateful use and discriminating acceptance of the critical work that has been done by biblical scholars during the last two centuries. I believe that there is need for more aids to Bible study for the general reader that are in this sense post-critical. In *Theology* recently a reviewer of books that aimed at meeting this need wrote as follows, and I agree with him: 'They obviously realize to how great an extent the "person in the pew" can conceive of nothing other than a literalist interpretation of the Bible, but feels unhappy with it, whereas no other approach to the Bible has ever been adequately, if at all, represented to him. As a result he rarely reads his Bible. Many "popular" books on the Bible and its use seem . . . to be written out of the conviction that it is actually undesirable "to present methods and achievements of New Testament scholarship to any interested layman", because this scholarship is assumed by their authors to be hostile to such a person's faith.'

However, while I hold that the fruits of modern scholarship nourish rather than inhibit faith, I have also drawn on the work of older, pre-critical expositors where they have in my view enlightened the meaning of the text or made noteworthy reflections upon it. I often refer to Matthew Henry's invaluable commentary on the whole Bible, which was produced in the seventeenth century. I was fortunate enough during the Second World War to buy for twelve shillings and sixpence a six-volume eighteenth-century folio edition of this work: the best bargain I have ever acquired.

My aim throughout has been to note points that should be of interest to the general reader of the Bible, not to provide all the information that is needed by academic students. I have avoided technical terms that the latter have to encounter such as 'eschatological', 'ontological', 'existential', etc.: I do not think they are likely ever to trip lightly off lay tongues. At the same time I incline to agree with the great scholar who said that the New Testament words always contain the most, not the least, possible meaning.

'I have sometimes seen more in a line of the Bible,' said Bunyan, 'than I could well tell how to stand under.'

ALEC VIDLER

Rye, April 1979

A Note on Bible Study Groups

There are many advantages to be derived from studying the Bible with other people as well as by oneself. A group of a dozen or fifteen people is large enough to contain a considerable variety of experience and points of view, and small enough to enable all the members to participate actively and to get to know one another well. Aldous Huxley, after attending a large conference, noted: 'Too many people. Cannot have very effective meeting over twelve; not for nothing limit fixed on twelve apostles.' The members of such a group can share with one another the points that each perceives or seizes, the questions or perplexities that strike some but not others, and each can contribute from his or her own experience or insight or reading what may be enlightening – or perhaps wholesomely disturbing – to the rest.

Anyone with a bit of enterprise can take an initiative in getting such a group together. It will be necessary to find a leader or convener or expositor who has had training in biblical studies in a college or university or otherwise, and can do the necessary homework and be ready at each meeting of the group to expound or comment on a passage of scripture, before all set to and discuss it. The expositor need not take the chair, and he need by no means be a minister of religion, though it is a thing that retired ministers or former divinity teachers in schools may be well qualified to do. They will need to be furnished with commentaries and other aids to study. The expositor cannot be expected to answer on the spot all the questions that will be raised, but he or she will know where to look for and find answers in so far as they are available, or be able to say that nobody has yet come up with a satisfactory explanation of this or that conundrum.

A Note on Bible Study Groups

The more mixed – within limits! – the membership of a Bible group is, the better. It should certainly be ecumenical in the sense of drawing its members from different denominations. Interested enquirers and doubters can also be included to the benefit of all. It is important that members should be regular in attendance, and not merely turn up occasionally. It should be borne in mind, when forming a group, that some people, who may have other excellent qualities, do not make good members of a study group: e.g. compulsive talkers who tend to monopolize a discussion, or fanatics (whether they be believers or unbelievers) who are not good listeners and not really open to learn from others. With that reservation, the more inclusive a group is, the more worthwhile membership of it is likely to prove.

All members must feel free and be encouraged to say just what they think; they must not be afraid of exposing their ignorance or their doubts; and they must be unshockable! There must be no holds barred. One advantage of the study group method is that, while it enables those who participate to discover more of the truth that the Bible contains than they would do if left to themselves, at the same time it prevents them from getting at the truth too easily or complacently. Unless the members are exceptionally dim or dumb, difficulties and obscurities and awkward questions of all sorts will be brought out and will have to be faced.

As regards practical details, I may outline a specimen method of conducting the proceedings of a Bible study group, which has been found to work well, but there is scope for much variety here. The group may meet either in one house or move around to the houses of different members according to who has convenient accommodation and accessibility. It is a good plan to start for five or ten minutes with a record of appropriate music. William Law in his *Serious Call* recommended people to begin their private devotions with the chanting of a psalm 'as something that is to awaken all that is good and holy within you,

11

that is to call your spirits to their proper duty . . . and to tune all the powers of your soul'. A similar purpose is served by beginning meetings of a study group with music. Incidentally, the music will also cover the entry of any members who may arrive a few minutes late.

A short prayer may then be said before the expositor proceeds to expound (i.e. to read and comment on) the passage of scripture selected. The expositor should have prepared beforehand and handed out slips of paper indicating texts elsewhere in the Bible that will be referred to and that different members of the group can then be ready to read when called upon. Every member of the group must of course possess a complete Bible, i.e. including the Apocrypha, and some may like to take notes for further study afterwards.

It is best to study one book in the Bible at a time and to go through it chapter by chapter and week by week, not just picking and choosing passages that look to be interesting or edifying. It is surprising how many questions can be started by apparently simple or straightforward or quite familiar statements. The exposition may take about half an hour. Then the matter is open for questioning, comment and discussion by all the members, and in a good and mature group no member will be too shy to participate. Sometimes, perhaps often, questions will come up which neither the expositor nor anyone else can answer at the moment: but researches can be made before the next meeting. Finally, there can be a closing prayer, such as 'The Grace', said together, and over tea and biscuits informal conversation will continue for as long as may be desired.

Introduction to Mark's Gospel

Mark's gospel has had a curious history and its popularity has fluctuated, as have the works of many other authors. It is now generally agreed that it is the earliest of the four gospels, though there are dissentient voices about this and there can be no absolute certainty concerning such a matter. Evidently this gospel won a quick prestige, since Matthew and Luke incorporated almost the whole of it in their gospels, with slight variations and in combination of course with much other material that they derived from other sources. A consequence was that before long Mark's gospel fell more or less into the shade and was less esteemed than the others. On the one hand, it came to be looked upon as a mere abridgement of Matthew; and on the other hand, since it contained hardly anything that was not in Matthew or Luke, why make much of it? This explains why very few of the liturgical gospels tradition-ally read at the communion service were taken from Mark, and also why early Christian writers seldom quoted from it or commented on it.

It was not until the nineteenth century that the import-ance and singularity of Mark's gospel were rediscovered. Critical scholarship demonstrated convincingly that it was the earliest of the gospels, a pioneer work. From this priority in date it was inferred that it was the most reli-able and the nearest to the facts that it records. The nine-teenth century also saw many attempts to write a bio-graphy of Jesus, and Mark's gospel easily came to be viewed as a biography, moreover as the biography that revealed most clearly the genuine humanity of Jesus. These latter inferences, popular as they were, were mistaken. A gospel is not a biography but a quite distinct kind of book, nor does it provide straightforward data for a biography, and Mark not only presupposes, but bears witness to, the divine character of Jesus as truly as the other evangelists do. So far from being a plain, matter-of-fact human story Mark's gospel is a much stranger and more mysterious book than may appear at first sight.

How did it come to be written? Jesus himself left nothing in writing, so far as we know. The apostles, at the start of their mission, felt no need for writings about the life of Jesus. Their interest was in the risen Lord, the living Christ, who would shortly be bringing God's purpose for mankind to fulfilment. Observe that the speeches attributed to Peter in the early chapters of Acts and the letters of Paul show no particular interest in the earthly life of Jesus. Since they did not expect human history to last for long there was no need to provide written evidence about Jesus for posterity. They could say all that needed to be said by word of mouth.

What then led to the production of documents and to the eventual composition of the gospels? First, there was the gradual fading of the expectation that the final consummation of all things was shortly to come to pass, so that writings would serve a useful purpose in the life of the Church and there was need to make provision for the future. Then again, there was the fact that as the Church moved further and further into the gentile world, converts and enquirers naturally wanted to know more about the events that had set the Christian mission in motion. So it came about that the stories about Jesus and his teaching, that the preachers and teachers were in the habit of telling by word of mouth, were by degrees written down, collected and circulated.

Originally these stories were separate units, not a continuous narrative: accounts either of the acts of Jesus (encounters, wonders, miracles) or of his teaching (parables, memorable pronouncements, etc.) that had been used and commented on by the preachers in their sermons. At this stage there was no interest in the chronology of the life of Jesus and no attempt was made to tell the stories in any correct historical order, though it seems that the account of his Passion and death assumed a fairly settled form before anything else: that is why our four gospels agree most closely when they reach that point in their narratives. Mark was apparently the first Christian to think of prefixing a collection of stories about the earthly ministry of Jesus to the already familiar record of the passion.

Who was this Mark? He may possibly have been the 'John Mark' who is mentioned elsewhere in the New Testament, and later tradition assumed that to be the case, but it was a common name at the time, so that we cannot be sure about his identity. It is however probable that he was a member of the church in Rome, and that his book was composed around A.D. 70 and originally designed for the use of the Christians there. There are various theories about why he arranged the stories about Jesus in the order that he did. He may have been influenced by the liturgical, catechetical or calendrical needs of the church. Ingenious scholars have proposed schemes that he may have been following, but none of them commands general assent. In any case Mark's object will have been to confirm and fortify the Christians in Rome in their faith, faced as they were with a hostile environment and with threatened or actual persecution. We know that there was a persecution of the church in Rome during the reign of the emperor Nero (A.D. 54-68). Mark was writing not for outsiders or for neophytes, but for the faithful, so he could take for granted that they would know who John the Baptist was, etc.

He was writing for people who believed that Jesus was the promised Messiah, but who were still puzzled by the fact that his career on earth had ended in complete disgrace and rejection and in a criminal's death. Mark meets this difficulty by showing that Jesus was really innocent of the charges that the Jewish authorities had brought against him, and also by indicating that it is God's way to produce great and glorious results from inconspicuous and inglorious beginnings.

Another question that Mark was concerned to answer was this: If Jesus was the Messiah, why had he not more openly asserted his claim to be so and why had his messiahship not been recognized? Mark's reply to this is in effect that Jesus kept his messiahship secret until the end because it would inevitably have been misunderstood. This is known as Mark's theory of the messianic secret.

It must be realized that messianic expectations took various forms.

(a) There was the expectation of a Davidic messiah, of a king in David's line who would restore the fortunes of Israel, shake off the oppressors, and lead the people to victory. For instance in a work known as the Psalms of Solomon (*c.* 50 B.C.) we read: 'Behold, o Lord, and raise up for them their king, the son of David . . . that he may reign over Israel thy servant. And gird him with strength to shatter unrighteous rulers, and to purge Jerusalem from Gentiles that trample her down to destruction . . . Happy are they that shall be born in these days, to see the good fortune of Israel which God will bring to pass.' This was the expectation of a political messiah.

(b) Alternatively, there was the hope of a levitical or priestly messiah. In the Testament of the Twelve Patriarchs (second century B.C.) we read: 'Then shall the Lord raise up a new priest, and to him all the words of the Lord shall be revealed . . . And he shall shine forth as the sun on the earth, and shall remove all darkness from under heaven . . .'

(c) There were also various kinds of apocalyptic or transcendental expectations of a Son of Man – see Daniel 7:13, and the Book of Enoch (first-second centuries B.C.): 'This is the Son of man who hath righteousness, with whom dwelleth righteousness, and who revealeth all the treasures of that which is hidden . . . The Lord of spirits hath chosen him.'

Mark had to show that, while Jesus did indeed fulfil the hopes of his people and came to them as God's final agent in the world, yet his messiahship differed in important respects from anything that had been expected. Above all, he was a Messiah who suffered and died for his people. In other words, the true Messiah is not one who triumphs in history and manifestly achieves the conquest of good over evil, but rather one who shows in his action and teaching that vicarious suffering, sacrificial service to the uttermost, is the final revelation of meaning in history. The ultimate triumph of love, the consummation of the kingdom of God, lies beyond history.

Again, Mark braces the Christians to face suffering and persecution by telling them how Jesus himself had suffered just as they were called to do, that he had clearly warned his followers to be prepared for these grave ordeals, and that he had promised sure rewards to those who were faithful.

The reader of Mark's gospel, in order to get its full flavour and effect, must try to forget what he knows from the later gospels. While it is true that comparison with the other gospels can bring home to us the distinct and unique characteristics of this one, an attempt should be made to respond to it as it was when it was the only gospel in the field. The gospels are to be regarded as portraiture, not as photography. One needs to concentrate all one's attention on a portrait by itself.

As regards Mark's style of writing, commentators have spoken of 'the ruthless brevity of the Marcan narrative that takes away the breath, even though we are accustomed to it' (Ca).[1] And again of 'the rough vigour and vividness of Mark's style. Mark is not a trained man of letters – indeed he often writes clumsily, inelegantly, ungrammatically – but he is one of those people who instinctively tell a story well' (Hu).

Other points that might well be mentioned in an introduction to the gospel will emerge as we consider it sec-

17

tion by section. I have from time to time hinted at questions that a study group might want to discuss, but the best questions are those that are evoked spontaneously, not put into people's minds.

[1] For list of abbreviations, see p. 173

The Gospel According to Mark

with notes and comments

The Gospel According to Mark

This is the title in the R.S.V. Some English translations more correctly render it just 'Mark's Version', for the Greek says no more than *According to Mark*, and even that was not there originally. The title was added some time in the second century. So the authorship was at first anonymous. The earliest Christian writers did not seek individual credit for their compositions, as most of us do nowadays. They were content to remain in the background, and anyhow the gospels are not purely individual compositions. They were the product of the corporate activity of a particular church or churches, in this case of the church in Rome.

1:1 *The beginning of the gospel of Jesus Christ, the Son of God* This seems to have been the original title either of the whole book or of the opening paragraph or section. Or the meaning may be as the New English Bible has it, 'Here begins the gospel of Jesus Christ . . .' *Gospel* means good news; it was not until later that the word came to be used for a written document or book, and then perhaps because Mark had used it as he does in this heading. However that may be, the book is to contain 'the good news about Jesus Christ'. It will certainly have come to its first readers as good news, whether they had been converted and baptized quite recently or several years ago. 'The word *gospel* would seem to have been very much at home in the vocabulary of the gentile mission, where it signified much more than a mere message or doctrine; it was used to describe that great evangelical movement of the Spirit which had its origin in Galilee and had spread as far as Rome' (Ca). But after nearly two thousand years can it still be good news in anything like the same way?

Jesus, which is the Greek form of Joshua, meaning saviour, was a common name among the Jews until the end of the second century A.D. *Christ*, on the other hand, is properly a title, meaning 'the anointed one', corresponding to 'Messiah' which means the same in Hebrew. In the New Testament it often has the definite article, *the Christ*, but it came to be used as if it were a name, as here by Mark. Some ancient authorities omit the words *the Son of God*. Mark could certainly have penned them. To a gentile Christian at Rome they would have meant a divine being, supernatural both in origin and power.

2 As it is written in Isaiah the prophet,

'Behold, I send my messenger before thy face,
who shall prepare thy way;
3 the voice of one crying in the wilderness:
Prepare the way of the Lord,
make his paths straight –'

4 John the baptizer appeared in the wilderness, preaching a baptism of repentance for the forgiveness of sins. 5 And there went out to him all the country of Judea, and all the people of Jerusalem; and they were baptized by him in the river Jordan, confessing their sins. 6 Now John was clothed with camel's hair, and had a leather girdle around his waist, and ate locusts and wild honey. 7 And he preached, saying, 'After me comes he who is mightier than I, the thong of whose sandals I am not worthy to stoop down and untie. 8 I have baptized you with water; but he will baptize you with the Holy Spirit.'

1:2f. The words quoted from the Old Testament in these verses show that the Messiah would be preceded by a forerunner, and then in 4f. Mark goes on to affirm that John the baptizer was the promised forerunner. The

Old Testament texts quoted are from Malachi 3:1 and Isaiah 40:3, though Mark attributes them both to Isaiah. This may be because the words from Malachi were added later, or because Mark was using a collection of O.T. texts or testimonies in which they were already combined. Such collections were certainly used by early Christian preachers. Note: often the New Testament writers used the Greek or Septuagint (LXX) version of the Old Testament which may differ in detail from the original Hebrew on which our English translations are based. So do not be surprised, when you look up O.T. quotations in your Bible, if you find that they do not correspond exactly with the wording in the N.T.

Prepare the way of the Lord . . . Matthew Henry, who has been described as 'the prince of biblical expositors', comments: 'Isaiah, the most evangelical of the prophets, begins the evangelical part of his prophecy with this, which points to the beginning of the gospel of Christ, Isaiah 40:3 "The voice of him that crieth in the wilderness".' And he adds: 'They that are sent to "prepare the way of the Lord", in such a vast howling wilderness as this is, have need to cry aloud, and not spare, and to lift up their voice like a trumpet.' Can it be said that those who are today called to prepare the way of the Lord, in what is in many respects a wilderness, do that? If not, why not?

1:4ff. It was believed on the basis of Malachi 4:5f. that the prophesied forerunner of the Messiah would be Elijah returned to earth. Mark believes that John had performed that office. So, to make the point, he says that John was clothed like Elijah (see 2 Kings 1:8). To the first readers of the gospel *a baptism of repentance for the forgiveness of sins* would recall a vividly remembered experience of their own. Many Christians today do not observe or even know the anniversary of their baptism. Is this reprehensible? When Mark says *all the country of Judea, and all the people of Jerusalem* went out to Jesus, he is no doubt indulging in a pardonable exaggeration. The point is that

John summoned the whole people to repent and make a fresh start. *Camel's hair* means a garment woven of camel's hair. Permission to eat *locusts* is given in Leviticus 11:20-23. They can be eaten either salted or roasted.

1:7f. These verses make it clear that John's role was purely preparatory. The stage is being set for the entry of the Messiah, though he will not be acknowledged as such by the human observers. Nevertheless, that Jesus is indeed the promised Messiah is to be shown now by the mysterious action of God and his Spirit.

9 In those days Jesus came from Nazareth of Galilee and was baptized by John in the Jordan. 10 And when he came up out of the water, immediately he saw the heavens opened and the Spirit descending upon him like a dove; 11 and a voice came from heaven, 'Thou art my beloved Son; with thee I am well pleased.'

1:9 *Jesus . . . was baptized by John* Mark records the baptism of Jesus without any hesitation. Later the fact that he was baptized, although he was not a sinner and did not need forgiveness, raised difficulties, which Matthew (3:14f.) tried to deal with in his gospel. We may take it that by being baptized Jesus was identifying himself with his people and dedicating himself to his messianic vocation. The Jewish expectation of the coming of a messianic deliverer, which took various forms (see p. 16 above), was based not only on Old Testament prophecy, but on the so-called apocalyptic literature that was current at the time. The word 'apocalypse' means 'unveiling' or 'revelation': apocalyptic writings purported to unveil things that were hidden or in the future. Daniel and the Revelation of John are apocalypses in the Bible.

1:10f. *He saw the heavens opened.* The vision is seen and the voice is heard by Jesus alone. This is in accord with Mark's theory of the messianic secret (see p. 16 above). 'The Christian in Rome, contemplating this vision, would think of his own baptism, in which he had received the same Spirit, and had become a son of God, crying aloud the words "Abba Father" (see Galatians 4:6)' (Ca). The Spirit is said to descend *like a dove*. The idea may be that as in Genesis 1:2 the Spirit is said to brood or hover over the face of the waters at the original creation, so when the Messiah comes, who is the mediator or inaugurator of a new creation, the Spirit broods over the waters of the Jordan in which he has been baptized. If so, this is a subtle indication that a new creation has now been set in motion. *'Thou are my beloved Son'* may mean 'my only Son'. In either case Jesus is secretly declared by God himself to be the expected Messiah.

12 The Spirit immediately drove him out into the wilderness. 13 And he was in the wilderness forty days, tempted by Satan; and he was with the wild beasts; and the angels ministered to him.

1:12f. *Tempted by Satan* The battle with the devil is joined at once. 'Satan' is a biblical name for 'the Adversary'. The Messiah was expected to be God's agent in overthrowing the powers of evil, and when he came there would be a great trial of strength between them. Mark means us to understand that, though the outcome will be victorious, the battle will continue throughout the ministry of Jesus, and indeed in the lives and experience of his followers. The true Church on earth is always to be a militant church. The *wilderness* was in those days regarded as a special home of evil spirits, and for obvious reasons. Where is the wilderness today? 'In the natural Desert of rocks and sands,' said Carlyle, 'or in the populous moral Desert of selfishness and baseness – to such Temptations are we all called . . . Our wilderness is the wide world in our Atheistic Century.' *Forty days* in the Bible is a conventional period of time, not to be taken literally. Moses was forty days and forty nights on the mount (see Exodus 34:28) and fasted throughout. While Mark says nothing about Jesus having fasted, he probably thought of him as 'the new Moses', the mediator of the new covenant: see note on 14:24 below. The *wild beasts*, one of the stage properties of the wilderness, may be mentioned to emphasize the loneliness and awfulness of the desert (see Isaiah 34:13f.). On the other hand, the wild beasts may be thought of as subject and friendly to Jesus in accordance with the Jewish belief that when Messiah came all animals would again be tame and live in harmony (see Hosea 2:18, Isaiah 11:6-9). *And the angels ministered to him.* In Psalm 91:11ff. dominion over the wild beasts is coupled with the service of angels, as here. There is this remarkable passage in the Testament of Naphtali: 'If you do good, my children, both men and angels shall bless you, and the devil shall flee from you and the wild beasts shall fear you and the Lord shall love you.' This is the background of Mark's description of the Lord's conflict with the powers of evil. Nowadays it would be put in more prosaic, but less telling, terms.

14 Now after John was arrested, Jesus came into Galilee, preaching the gospel of God, 15 and saying, 'The time is fulfilled, and the kingdom of God is at hand; repent, and believe in the gospel.'

The messianic herald has appeared, and the Messiah himself has been secretly designated by God and, behind the scenes as it were, has engaged in the crucial conflict with the powers of evil. It is time now for him to enter on his public ministry and to enlist his first followers.

1:14 *Now after John was arrested* The forerunner has done his work and he makes way for Jesus. Later on (in Chapter 6) Mark will tell the story of John's death in prison. *The gospel of God* can mean either the good news about God or the good news from God. By the time Mark wrote it was a well-known expression.

1:15 *The time is fulfilled* i.e. the designated time, the favourable time, the opportune time, the time of crisis, the time of which John spoke in v. 8. This time has arrived. *The kingdom of God* means God actively reigning and ruling over the world and over his people. A new age is dawning in which God's kingship is to be realized in a new way. As Alan Richardson put it, 'in general terms this means that Jesus proclaimed as good news the fact that God was setting about the task of putting straight the evil plight into which the world had fallen, or that he was beginning to bring to its fulfilment his original intention in the Creation.' It is through his followers, who will comprise his Church, that he wills to implement this task. Though the Church is not identical with the kingdom, it was well said by A. Loisy that Jesus proclaimed the kingdom and it was the Church that came. The Church, as Emil Brunner said, 'is a visible adumbration of the kingdom of God', and an adumbration has been defined as 'a faint sketch'. The kingdom was not to be fully realized in the near future as was supposed at first, but the Church was to witness till the end of time by its words and actions to its reality. *Is at hand* i.e. is now being inaugurated. *Repent* means more than penitence for sin and more than a change of mind; it involves a complete reorientation of the personality, i.e. a conversion.

16 And passing along by the Sea of Galilee, he saw Simon and Andrew the brother of Simon casting a net in the sea; for they were fishermen. 17 And Jesus said to them, 'Follow me and I will make you become fishers of men.' 18 And immediately they left their nets and followed him. 19 And going on a little farther, he saw James the son of Zebedee and John his brother, who were in their boat mending the nets. And immediately he called them; and they left their father Zebedee in the boat with the hired servants, and followed him.

These first four disciples constituted the Church in embryo. The same call is addressed to all Mark's readers, and their response ought to be equally prompt and unconditional, though if we are to believe the fourth gospel the Lord's summons was not so abrupt as it is here. All Christians are called to assist Jesus in catching men, i.e. in drawing them out of the turbulent waters of this old world into the life of the age to come, and this may entail giving up both means of livelihood and the closest natural ties, as it did in the case of the first disciples. Mankind is always in deep waters and in the dark: Jesus calls apostles to work with him in bringing freedom and enlightenment to others.

1:16 *They were fishermen* On this M. Henry comments: 'The instruments Christ chose to employ in setting up his kingdom were the weak and foolish things of the world; not called from the great Sanhedrin, or the schools of the Rabbins, but picked up from among the tarpaulins by the seaside, that the excellency of the power might appear to be wholly of God, and not at all of men.'

1:17 *Fishers of men* The metaphor is a familiar one in the O.T. 'Thou makest men like the fish of the sea': Habbakuk 1:14f. See also Jeremiah 16:16; Ezekiel 29:4f.; Amos 4:2.

1:18 The observant reader will already have noticed that *immediately* is one of Mark's favourite words, which he used somewhat indiscriminately. While it may seem to give his narrative 'an air of breathlessness', it is perhaps better regarded as an engaging mannerism. 'It was obviously a conventional mannerism, like the Welsh "look you"' (Ca).

1:20 *With the hired servants* Is this the reminiscence of an eyewitness or an indication that James and John did not completely abandon their aged father? It used to be thought that Mark's gospel incorporated the reminiscences of Peter. While that is too definite and unverifiable a supposition, much in the gospel story must derive in one way or another from the testimony of eyewitnesses.

21 And they went into Capernaum, and immediately on the sabbath he entered the synagogue and taught.

22 and they were astonished at his teaching, for he taught them as one who had authority, and not as the scribes. 23 And immediately there was in their synagogue a man with an unclean spirit; 24 and he cried out. 'What have you to do with us, Jesus of Nazareth? Have you come to destroy us? I know who you are, the Holy One of God.' 25 But Jesus rebuked him, saying, 'Be silent, and come out of him!' 26 And the unclean spirit, convulsing him and crying with a loud voice, came out of him. 27 And they were all amazed, so that they questioned among themselves, saying, 'What is this? A new teaching! With authority he commands even the unclean spirits, and they obey him.' 28 And at once his fame spread everywhere throughout all the surrounding region of Galilee.

This may be seen as a typical day's activity in Capernaum on the north-west shore of the lake, which according to Mark was the centre of Jesus's activity.

1:21 *He entered the synagogue* The synagogue in each place corresponded roughly to our parish churches. The sabbath services were not unlike the anglican mattins and evensong: prayers, praises, and readings from scripture, with a sermon that any qualified Israelite might be asked to give. On weekdays the synagogue served as a school. *And taught* Mark tells us little about *what* Jesus taught (in comparison with Matthew, Luke or John), but he does tell us *how* he taught and the impression that he made.

1:22 *As one who had authority, and not as the scribes* That is to say, he did not depend on ancient texts or appeal to rabbis greater or older than himself. His message seemed to come direct from God. 'Christ was a non-such preacher; he did not preach as the scribes, who expounded the law of Moses by rote as a school boy saith his lesson' (H). 'Many scribes indeed there have been, and are, possessed of human learning . . .: but our prayer ought to be, that "scribes, well instructed unto the kingdom of God", may teach with authority in all congregations after the manner of Christ; and to the conviction and astonishment of such hearers as have hitherto been taught in a mere formal manner; and this would render our churches more frequented than they now generally are' (Sc).

1:23 Not only did Jesus speak with authority, but he acted with authority against the powers of evil; and the powers of evil, to whom supernatural knowledge is ascribed, recognized him as Messiah when healthy human beings didn't. *An unclean spirit* means an evil or vicious spirit or a demon. Mental illness was so conceived and described in those days. Are modern psychological descriptions more expressive? The stories about the casting out of demons, which figure prominently in Mark's gospel, lead, as someone has said, 'into that strange twilight zone in the ancient world between medicine and magic which is appropriately described by the word "thaumaturgy" '. Their meaning for us, as indeed for the first readers of the gospel, is that they testify to the sovereign power of God at work in Jesus, which can overcome all the evils by which, under whatever nomenclature, mankind is as much afflicted now as in the first century. Jesus is not simply one exorcist among others, but the One who is to bring about the final destruction of the demonic powers that are hostile to God.

1:24 *What have you to do with us?* i.e. 'Why are you interfering with us?' *Have you come to destroy us?* This could be an assertion: 'You have come to destroy us.' *The Holy One of God* i.e. the Messiah. The evil spirit recognizes Jesus as Messiah, while the bystanders don't. The demons can penetrate the messianic secret.

1:25 *Be silent*=Be muzzled: a formula used in the ancient world for exorcism. 'Christ has a muzzle for that unclean spirit, when he fawns, as well as when he barks' (H).

1:27f. Mark gives a vivid impression of the natural and incoherent remarks of the crowd. Moffat well translates: 'They were all so amazed that they discussed it together, saying, "Whatever is this?" "It's new teaching with authority behind it!" "He orders even unclean spirits!" "Yes, and they obey him!".'

29 And immediately he left the synagogue, and entered the house of Simon and Andrew, with James and John. 30 Now Simon's mother-in-law lay sick with a fever, and immediately they told him of her. 31 And he came and took her by the hand and lifted her up, and the fever left her; and she served them.

We have seen how the messianic power of Jesus could deal with a case of demonic possession, i.e. with mental illness; now we are to see that it can also deal with other forms of sickness.

1:30 *They told him of her*, perhaps to excuse her non-appearance, rather than asking him to cure her. The duty of entertaining guests would devolve upon the mother-in-law, especially if Peter was a widower.

1:31 *And she served them* i.e. at table. The words show the completeness of the cure. St Jerome commented: 'The human constitution is such that after fever our bodies are rather tired, but when the Lord bestows health restoration is immediate and complete.'

32 That evening, at sundown, they brought to him all who were sick or possessed with demons. 33 And the whole city was gathered together about the door. 34 And he healed many who were sick with various diseases, and cast out many demons; and he would not permit the demons to speak, because they knew him.

The cures described here show that the two cases just mentioned were not freaks or coincidences, but instances of the healing power that was regularly exercised by Jesus.

1:32 *That evening, at sundown* i.e. when the sabbath was over and it was permitted to bring the sufferers through the streets. *Brought to him all . . . and he healed many* Matthew (8:16) transposes 'all' and 'many' to avoid giving the

31

impression that some were not cured.

1.34 *He would not permit the demons to speak, because they knew him* i.e. knew who he was. They are forbidden to betray the messianic secret.

35 And in the morning, a great while before day, he rose and went out to a lonely place, and there he prayed. 36 And Simon and those who were with him pursued him, 37 and they found him and said to him, 'Every one is searching for you.' 38 And he said to them, 'Let us go on to the next towns, that I may preach there also; for that is why I came out.' 39 And he went throughout all Galilee, preaching in their synagogues and casting out demons.

Jesus extends his ministry to other places. His motive for leaving Capernaum may have been that the results of his ministry there seem to have been excitement and amazement, not the enlistment of followers or converts: so he goes to seek them elsewhere.

1:35 *In the morning, a great while before day, he rose* 'I take it for granted,' wrote William Law, 'that every Christian that is in health is up early in the morning; for it is much more reasonable to suppose a person up early because he is a Christian than because he is a labourer or a tradesman or a servant or has business that wants him . . . How much is he to be reproved that had rather lie folded up in a bed than be raising up his heart to God in acts of praise and adoration.' But is this so?

1:38 *That is why I came* Does this mean from Capernaum or from heaven to earth, which is how Luke (4:43) takes it? Cp. Weymouth's translation here: 'for that purpose I came from God'.

40 And a leper came to him beseeching him, and kneeling said to him, 'If you will, you can make me clean.' 41 Moved with pity, he stretched out his hand and touched him, and said to him, 'I will; be clean.'

42 And immediately the leprosy left him, and he was made clean. 43 And he sternly charged him, and sent him away at once, 44 and said to him, 'See that you say nothing to any one; but go, show yourself to the priest, and offer for your cleansing what Moses commanded, for a proof to the people.' 45 But he went out and began to talk freely about it, and to spread the news, so that Jesus could no longer openly enter a town, but was out in the country; and people came to him from every quarter.

Even leprosy, which was the most dreaded and disfiguring of diseases, yielded to the power of Jesus. It involved ritual uncleanness and segregation from society. The Jewish law did nothing for lepers; it merely sought to protect the rest of the community from them. Is that our attitude now to the violent, to hooligans, to criminals?

1:41 *Moved with pity* Probably the correct reading is 'moved with anger', and an early copyist altered it to 'pity'. What made Jesus angry? Perhaps it is his reaction to the combined forces of death, disease, sin and Satan. *And touched him* This would have seemed at the time an unthinkable action.

1:43 *Go, show yourself to the priest* in accordance with Leviticus 14:1-5, where elaborate directions about the treatment of lepers are prescribed. *For a proof to the people* i.e. as evidence that he is now fit to be received back into human society.

1:45 *Jesus could no longer openly enter a town* Perhaps just 'town', i.e. Capernaum. He wants to avoid a popular agitation and the reputation of being only a wonder-worker.

2:1 And when he returned to Capernaum after some days, it was reported that he was at home. 2 And many were gathered together, so that there was no longer room for them, not even about the door; and he was preaching the word to them. 3 And they came, bringing to him a paralytic carried by four men. 4 And when they could not get near him because of the crowd, they removed the roof above him; and when they had made an opening, they let down the pallet on which the paralytic lay. 5 And when Jesus saw their faith, he said to the paralytic, 'My son, your sins are forgiven.' 6 Now some of the scribes were sitting there, questioning in their hearts, 7 'Why does this man speak thus? It is blasphemy! Who can forgive sins but God alone?' 8 And immediately Jesus, perceiving in his spirit that they thus questioned within themselves, said to them, 'Why do you question thus in your hearts? 9 Which is easier, to say to the paralytic, "Your sins are forgiven", or to say, "Rise, take up your pallet and walk"? 10 But that you may know that the Son of man has authority on earth to forgive sins' – he said to the paralytic – 11 'I say to you, rise, take up your pallet and go home.' 12 And he rose, and immediately took up the pallet and went out before them all; so that they were all amazed and glorified God, saying, 'We never saw anything like this!'

From 2:1 to 3:6 Mark narrates a series of incidents that illustrate the increasing hostility of the Jewish authorities to Jesus. While the common people heard him gladly, their leaders, motivated by jealousy or concern for their own power, sought to challenge his authority. These episodes have been described as a collection of 'conflict stories'. Mark means his readers to understand that the opposition to Jesus was unwarranted and due to misunderstanding.

The first of these stories (2:1-12) appears to be a combination of two different episodes, the healing of a paralytic and a discussion about forgiveness, which Mark or the source on which he was depending has rather awkwardly joined together: e.g. consider the awkwardness of v. 10. In fact, if we omit vv. 5b to 10a as an insertion dealing with forgiveness, the healing of the paralytic makes perfectly good sense by itself. On the other hand, the evangelist is no doubt right in seeing a connection between restoration to health and the forgiveness of sin.

2:1 *He was at home* may mean that he was in the house of Simon and Andrew or simply that he was 'indoors'.

2:2 *Many were gathered together* 'many of them perhaps came only for cures, and many perhaps only for curiosity to get a sight of him; but when he had them together he preached to them. Tho' the synagogue was open to him at proper times, he thought it not at all amiss to preach in a house on a weekday' (H).

2:3 *And they came* Who are *they*? The parents of the paralytic?

2:4 *They removed the roof above him* It would be a house with a flat roof and an outside staircase. 'The roof was probably formed by beams and rafters, across which matting, branches and twigs, covered with earth trodden hard, were laid. To make an aperture large enough for the bed would not be difficult' (T). *The pallet* The Greek word so translated signifies a poor man's bed or mattress.

2:5 As the story stands, Jesus is represented as ascribing the man's physical condition to sin and thus as regarding forgiveness or absolution as his primary need. He may indeed have recognized such a connection, though elsewhere in the gospels it is made clear that he did not hold that sin was the only cause of illness or disaster (see Luke 13: 1-5; John 9: 1f.).

2:6 *Questioning in their hearts* We should say 'in their minds': see note on 3:5. This is the first hint of opposition to Jesus.

2:7 *It is blasphemy!* Forgiveness of sin was regarded as the prerogative of God (see e.g. Isaiah 43:25; 44:22), and Jesus was therefore charged with usurping a divine right. *Blasphemy* means an affront to the majesty of God.

2:10 *The Son of man* There is a very extensive literature about the background and meaning of this expression, which is used by Jesus himself in the gospels, but hardly ever elsewhere in the New Testament. A possible explanation, that suits the present context, is that Jesus used it as a concealed or enigmatic way of affirming his messiahship which was not understood at the time. In that case, it will mean here that, as God's representative or agent on earth, he has authority to forgive sins, which is indeed a divine prerogative. The forgiveness of sin as well as the healing of disease were evidence that the reign of God had drawn near. This discussion about forgiveness need not have taken place as early in the ministry as Mark's arrangement of his material may lead the reader to suppose.

13 He went out again beside the sea; and all the crowd gathered about him, and he taught them. 14 And as he passed on, he saw Levi the son of Alphaeus sitting at the tax office, and he said to him, 'Follow me'. And he rose and followed him.

The call of Levi is narrated as a lead into the account of Jesus's relations with social outcasts, and possibly because Mark's readers in Rome had a special interest in him.

2:13 *Levi* is not included in Mark's list of the twelve apostles (3:16-19), but Matthew (9:9; 10:3) identifies him with Matthew and so makes him one of the twelve.

2:14 *The tax office* This customs office or toll house would be situated on the frontier between the territories of Herod Philip and Herod Antipas. Customs officials or tax collectors (called 'publicans' in the Authorized Version) had a bad reputation for rapacity and petty extortions; also because they mixed with non-Jews. Levi presumably was in the service of Herod Antipas, but in Judea and Samaria the tax officials worked for the Romans and so were regarded as 'quislings'.

15 And as he sat at the table in his house, many tax collectors and sinners were sitting with Jesus and his

disciples; for there were many who followed him. 16
And the scribes of the Pharisees, when they saw that he
was eating with sinners and tax collectors, said to his
disciples, 'Why does he eat with tax collectors and sinners?' 17 And when Jesus heard it, he said to them,
'Those who are well have no need of a physician, but
those who are sick; I came not to call the righteous, but
sinners.'

Jesus did not avoid sinners, as strict Jews did, but sought
them out and associated with them. In the early Church
there was a lively interest in questions about table-fellow-
ship (see Acts 11:3; Galatians 2:12).

2:15 *In his house* Presumably Levi's house, though
some have thought that Jesus was the host. *And sinners*
This might mean disreputable people in general, but more
probably people who did not observe the Jewish law according to pharisaic standards. Cp. John 7:49: 'This
crowd, who do not know the law, are accursed.' *For
there were many who followed him* i.e. many more than
those whose conversion has been narrated.

2:16 *The scribes of the Pharisees* A curious expression
which must mean scribes who belonged to the party of
the Pharisees, implying that other scribes belonged to the
rival party of the Sadducees. The derivation of the name
'Pharisee' is disputed. They punctiliously observed the
law including the oral traditions, and in contrast to the
Sadducees believed in an after life. In the gospels they
do not appear in a favourable light because of their
legalism, but 'it is important to recognize their real rela-
tive goodness. In the time of Jesus they were the real
spiritual leaders of the nation . . . Jesus certainly had
more in common with them than with the Sadducees' (Cr).
Why does he eat with tax collectors and sinners? To the
Pharisees it was repulsive to eat with such people because of their laxity about the food regulations.

2:17 This is a proverbial saying. A physician can
hardly do anything for the sick if he avoids contact with

them. The mission of Jesus is to the disreputable, not to the respectable. 'The greatest of all disorders,' said Thomas Wilson, 'is to think we are whole, and need no help.' How does the contemporary Church fare under this test?

18 Now John's disciples and the Pharisees were fasting; and people came and said to him, 'Why do John's disciples and the disciples of the Pharisees fast, but your disciples do not fast?' 19 And Jesus said to them, 'Can the wedding guests fast while the bridegroom is with them? As long as they have the bridegroom with them, they cannot fast. 20 The days will come, when the bridegroom is taken away from them, and then they will fast in that day. 21 No one sews a piece of unshrunk cloth on an old garment; if he does, the patch tears away from it, the new from the old, and a worse tear is made. 22 And no one puts wine into old wineskins; if he does, the wine will burst the skins, and the wine is lost, and so are the skins; but new wine is for fresh skins.'

There were questions and controversies about fasting in the early Church and this passage may be designed to answer the question: Why do Christians fast if Jesus didn't? But the exact meaning is far from clear, and these verses have been interpreted in various ways.

2:18 *John's disciples and the Pharisees* The question may have originated in the period after the death of John when his disciples were observing a fast in mourning for him. In this case, the Pharisees may have been brought into the picture later. Jesus was asked why his disciples were not fasting as John's were, and his parabolic answer (v. 19) meant that they still had their Master with them and so had no occasion to mourn his loss. But the question could also have had to do with the different attitudes to asceticism of Jesus and John (see Matthew 11:18f.) rather than with a mourning fast.

2:20 This verse may be an addition to Jesus's original

answer. It is the first foreboding in this gospel that he is destined to meet a fate like that of John. The figure of the bridegroom may imply a secret or enigmatic claim on the part of Jesus to be the Messiah.

2:21f. These two verses were originally an independent unit. The two little parables have to do with the relation between the old and the new. We cannot tell what was the original context in which Jesus spoke them. The point seems to be that the new gospel is incompatible with the old order (pharisaic Judaism), and the new message must express itself through a new medium. A new patch tears a garment by shrinking and pulling the surrounding threads. Wineskins grew brittle in time, and fresh grape juice as it fermented would easily burst them. 'New skins for new wine' may have been a proverbial saying.

Christians nowadays seem largely to have abandoned the practice of fasting. Asceticism is out of fashion. Is this as it should be? Mahatma Gandhi said that 'all restraint, whatever prompts it, is wholesome for man', and many religious leaders have said much the same. Were they wrong?

23 One sabbath he was going through the grainfields; and as they made their way his disciples began to pluck heads of grain. 24 And the Pharisees said to him, 'Look, why are they doing what is not lawful on the sabbath?' 25 And he said to them, 'Have you never read what David did, when he was in need and was hungry, he and those who were with him: 26 how he entered the house of God, when Abiathar was high priest, and ate the bread of the Presence, which it is not lawful for any but the priests to eat, and also gave it to those who were with him?' 27 And he said to them, 'The Sabbath was made for man, not man for the sabbath; 28 so the Son of man is lord even of the sabbath.'

The connection between fasting and being hungry may have led Mark to place this incident here. When the gospel was written, the sabbath was not observed by gentile Christians, and so this anecdote and the one that follows it will have been appreciated by them as justifying their freedom.

2:23 This must have been in April-June if the corn was to be pluckable. It is the only clear reference in Mark to the season of the year, except for the final Passover. In Deuteronomy 23:25 we read: 'When you go into your neighbour's standing grain, you may pluck the ears with your hand, but you shall not put a sickle to your neighbour's standing grain.' However, to pluck on a sabbath was equivalent to reaping and so was forbidden activity. Henry quaintly comments: 'What a poor breakfast Christ's disciples had on a sabbath-day morning, when they were going to church . . . They were so intent upon spiritual dainties, that they forgot their necessary food.'

2:24 'It is idle to ask what *the Pharisees* were doing in the middle of a cornfield on a sabbath day . . . Scribes or Pharisees appear or disappear just as the compiler requires them' (N). They are required here since, as we have seen, this is one of a series of stories that illustrates Jesus's conflicts with the Jewish authorities.

2:25 *Have you never read . . .?* This is a kind of argument that would appeal to the rabbinic mind. It is to say: 'For the sake of argument let us allow the validity of the law: still there are exceptions to it. Take the case of that greatly respected figure, King David.'

2:26 *The house of God*=the Tabernacle. In I Samuel 21 it is not Abiathar but Ahimelech who was the high priest. This must have been a slip on Mark's part. Matthew and Luke in reproducing the story omit the name since they realized that it was wrong. For *the bread of the Presence* (A.V.: 'shew-bread') see Leviticus 24:5-9. The argument is that since scripture did not condemn David for what he did on this occasion, the rigid pharisaic interpretation of the law was unwarranted. 'Ritual observances must give way to moral obligations; and that may be done in a case of necessity, which otherwise may not be done' (H).

2:27 *The sabbath was made for man* . . . This is a further argument, appealing to a wider principle, namely that the law is for man, not man for the law, an argument that cuts the ground from under every form of legalism. 'The sabbath was made for the whole human race . . . not only for the Jew . . . It is like the sun, a universal blessing' (R. M. McCheyne).

2:28 *The Son of man* could here mean just 'man'; but this verse is probably a Christian comment that was added to the story, meaning that the Son of man, i.e. the Messiah, is Lord even in respect of the sabbath. The Pharisees stood for what came to be known as sabbatarianism, which still had a considerable hold in Britain in the nineteenth century, witness Mrs Proudie and Mr Slope in *Barchester Towers*. Has the reaction now gone too far, and is the time ripe for a reconsideration of the value of observing the Lord's day, which is not of course the same as the Jewish sabbath? In what respects is it, or could it be, a universal blessing, like the sun?

3:1 Again he entered the synagogue, and a man was there who had a withered hand. 2 And they watched him, to see whether he would heal him on the sabbath, so that they might accuse him. 3 And he said to the man who had the withered hand, 'Come here.' 4 And he said to them, 'Is it lawful on the sabbath to do good or to do harm, to save life or to kill?' But they were silent. 5 And he looked around at them with anger, grieved at their hardness of heart, and said to the man, 'Stretch out your hand.' He stretched it out, and his hand was restored. 6 The Pharisees went out, and immediately held counsel with the Herodians against him, how to destroy him.

This is the fifth in the series of stories designed to illustrate the conflict between Jesus and the Jewish authorities. Like the preceding one it concerns sabbath observance, but here it is not the disciples but Jesus himself who is charged with breaking the sabbath.

3:1 *Again he entered the synagogue* i.e. on another occasion. No place is indicated but it may be implied that it was the synagogue in Capernaum. *A man . . . with a withered hand* i.e. a paralysed hand. St Jerome says that the (apocryphal) Gospel According to the Hebrews described the man as a mason, who depended on the use of his hands for his livelihood and who said to Jesus, 'I pray thee to restore me mine health, that I may not beg for my food.'

3:2 *And they* (i.e. the Pharisees) *watched him* The question in their minds was: will he heal? Healing was regarded as work. The rabbinical rule was that relief might be given to sufferers on the sabbath only when life was in danger, which was not the case here.

3:3 *Come here* i.e. stand up and come where you can be seen.

3:4 *Is it lawful on the sabbath to do good . . .?* or 'Are we allowed to do good . . .?' (We). The point of the question asked by Jesus is not as obvious as may be supposed. Does it mean: 'Is it right for me to heal this man or to refrain from healing him? Not to do the good to him that I can do would be to do him evil.' Or does it mean: 'Which course of action is right – what I am going to do to preserve this man's life or what you are planning to do to compass my death (see v. 6)?' *But they were silent* They could not think what to say.

3:5 *And he looked around at them with anger* because of their evasiveness when confronted with a question of life and death. Matthew and Luke thought *anger* was too strong an emotion to attribute to Jesus, and so omitted it when they reproduced this story. But there is such a thing as righteous anger: pictures of the gentle Jesus 'meek and mild' can be very misleading, as in some stained glass windows, etc. *Grieved at their hardness of heart* In the

Bible the heart was the seat of understanding, not of affection as with us. What is meant here is their blind obtuseness or insensibility or their obstinate stupidity.

3:6 This verse is intended to be the conclusion not only of this story but of the series of five conflicts with the Jewish authorities. They show the grounds on which the religious and secular authorities eventually combined to destroy Jesus. *The Herodians*, who were the friends and supporters of Herod Antipas, represent the latter. It was a combination of ecclesiastics and influential laymen. Mark implies that from this point there was a definite breach between Jesus and official Judaism. He left the synagogue never to return, except once at Nazareth, his home town (6:1-6). *How to destroy him* 'As a dark cloud the death of Jesus hangs over the further course of his ministry.'

7 Jesus withdrew with his disciples to the sea, and a great multitude from Galilee followed; and also from Judea 8 and Jerusalem and Idumea and from beyond the Jordan and from about Tyre and Sidon a great multitude, hearing all that he did, came to him. 9 And he told his disciples to have a boat ready for him because of the crowd, lest they should crush him; 10 for he had healed many, so that all who had diseases pressed upon him to touch him. 11 And whenever the unclean spirits beheld him, they fell down before him and cried out, 'You are the Son of God.' 12 And he strictly ordered them not to make him known.

This paragraph did not reach Mark as an independent unit, but was composed by the evangelist himself. It indicates that at this point Jesus, having withdrawn from the synagogue, adopted a change of tactics in his ministry. Having broken with, and having been rejected by, the old Israel, he takes steps to create a new community of God's people, a new Israel, and in the next section (vv. 13-19) he will appoint its leaders.

3:7 *A great multitude . . . followed* The Greek text

here is uncertain. It seems probable that the word 'followed' should be omitted (see N.E.B.), so that only one crowd is depicted, drawn from all parts of the Holy Land inhabited by Jews. Note that Samaria is conspicuously excluded. It is out of all these people that Jesus is going to form the new community of his followers.

3:9 *Have a boat ready* The mention of the boat here prepares the way for the lakeside teaching in 4:1ff. It is to be at the disposal of Jesus, so that he can avoid the pressure of the crowd.

3:10 *All who had diseases* The word here translated 'diseases' literally means 'scourges'. It was a conventional synonym for disease and need not imply the idea that illness is a punishment for sin.

3:11 *The unclean spirits . . . fell down before him* The actions of the demoniacs are attributed by Mark to the demons who possess them. As elsewhere, since they have supernatural knowledge, they recognize Jesus as Messiah.

3:12 But in accordance with Mark's theory of the messianic secret they are enjoined to be silent about it.

13 And he went up on the mountain, and called to him those whom he desired; and they came to him. 14 And he appointed twelve, to be with him, and to be sent out to preach 15 and have authority to cast out demons: 16 Simon whom he surnamed Peter 17 James the son of Zebedee and John the brother of James, whom he surnamed Boanerges, that is, sons of thunder; 18 Andrew, and Philip, and Bartholomew, and Matthew, and Thomas, and James the son of Alphaeus, and Thaddaeus, and Simon the Cananaean, 19 and Judas Iscariot, who betrayed him.

3:13 *He went up on the mountain* The correct translation is 'into the mountain' (as in R.V. and Go). This was the traditional setting for a solemn, divine act. Cp. Moses on Mount Sinai and the Sermon on the Mount. In other words, this is a theological, not a topographical, statement. *And called to him those whom he desired; and they came to him.* The initiative of Jesus is emphasized and also the immediate response of those called. It seems to be implied that he called to him a large number from whom he chose twelve.

3:14 *And he appointed twelve* There is no disagreement about the number twelve, but if the names of the apostles listed in the gospels and Acts are compared, there is divergence about some. Some appear to have played little part in the life of the early Church, so that there could be doubt about their identity. The twelve are the foundation members of the new people of God, of the new Israel. The old Israel was a twelve-fold body (the twelve tribes), and the new Israel follows suit. *To be with him, and to be sent out* They are to be in constant association with him as disciples with their master and to have a mission such as Mark is going to describe in chapter 6.

3:16 *Simon whom he surnamed Peter* When did Jesus give him this name which means 'rock'? There is no clear answer. The name was given not because Peter had a rock-like character but because of the part he was to play as spokesman and representative of the twelve.

3:17 *Boanerges* is an obscure word of which the meaning is uncertain. It might mean that James and John were of a thundery disposition or that they were twins. 'Perhaps', conjectured Matthew Henry, 'they were remarkable for a loud commanding voice, they were thundering preachers; or rather, it notes the zeal and fervency of their spirits, which would make them active for God above their brethren. These two (saith Dr Hammond) were to be special eminent ministers of the gospel, which is called a voice shaking the earth. Hebrews 12:26.'

3:18 *Simon the Cananaean* i.e. of the Zealot party as the extreme nationalists came to be known.

3:19 *Judas Iscariot* 'Iscariot' probably means 'man of Kerioth' (a place name). The suggestion that it derives from *sicarius* (assassin) is unlikely. It may already have been unintelligible to Mark and that is why he leaves it unexplained.

19b Then he went home; 20 and the crowd came together again, so that they could not even eat. 21 And when his family heard it, they went out to seize him, for people were saying, 'He is beside himself.' 22 And the scribes who came down from Jerusalem said, 'He is possessed by Beelzebub, and by the prince of demons he casts out the demons.' 23 And he called them to him, and said to them in parables, 'How can Satan cast out Satan? 24 If a kingdom is divided against itself, that kingdom cannot stand. 25 And if a house is divided against itself, that house will not be able to stand. 26 And if Satan has risen up against himself and is divided, he cannot stand, but is coming to an end. 27 But no one can enter a strong man's house and plunder his goods, unless he first binds the strong man; then indeed he may plunder his house.'

3:19b *Then he went home* Perhaps to the house of Simon and Andrew, or it may mean simply 'he went indoors'. In this passage Mark is going to contrast the way in which Jesus was welcomed by the ordinary people with the hostility of the religious leaders and even of his friends or family, who would not acknowledge the true source of his power but attributed it to evil sources. We are reminded of the Johannine saying: 'he came unto his own and his own received him not' (John 1:11).

3:20 *So that they could not even eat* 'so that there was no opportunity for them even to snatch a meal' (We). A.V. and R.V. have 'could not even eat bread', a literally correct translation that led M. Henry to remark that they 'could not get time *so much as to eat bread*, much less for a set and full meal'! But the R.S.V. translation is right, since the expression covered taking food of any kind.

3:21 *His family* The Greek means 'those with him',

which some commentators take to mean his family and others his friends. For the unbelief of members of Jesus's family, cp. John 7:5. '*He is beside himself*' can also be translated 'he must be mad', 'he is out of his mind', or 'he has taken leave of his senses'. The words describe a state of dangerous mental exaltation (cp. 2 Corinthians 5:13).

3:22 *The scribes who came down from Jerusalem* They would have greater prestige and authority than the provincial ones. It is implied that they came down especially to observe and report on what was going on in Galilee. *He is possessed by Beelzebub. Beelzebul* is a more likely spelling of this obscure word. Mark seems to regard it as an alternative name for Satan. *Beelzebul* has been taken to mean either 'Lord of dung' (*dung* being an opprobrious name for idols) or 'Lord of the house', which the metaphor of the house in vv. 23 and 27 may favour.

3:23 *Said to them in parables* 'Parables' (see also note on 4:1-9) are illustrations, which may be stories or aphorisms or picturesque sayings. The point Jesus is making here is that whereas the devil is the author of madness, disease and falsehood, he himself is working to produce just the opposite effects, namely health and healing. Thus in ascribing his work to the devil, the scribes are making the absurd assertion that the devil is pursuing two directly opposite policies.

3:26 If Satan had really risen up against himself, then he would not be able to stand and would be finished, whereas in point of fact he is evidently still strong.

3:27 This is a proverbial saying distinct from those that precede. You cannot rob a strong man unless you have first overpowered him and tied him up, but Jesus by his healings and exorcisms was clearly robbing the devil: so the devil had been bound by one who was stronger than he.

28 'Truly, I say to you, all sins will be forgiven the sons of men, and whatever blasphemies they utter; 29 but whoever blasphemes against the Holy Spirit never

has forgiveness, but is guilty of an eternal sin' — 30 for they had said, 'He has an unclean spirit.'

These verses are prefaced by the word 'Amen', which signifies that they are to be regarded as especially solemn. They have always puzzled Christians and have been a source of anguish to many who have supposed that they may have committed the 'unforgivable sin'. To any who are beset by this fear it can be said with confidence that the fact that they are concerned about the question is a sure sign that they have not done so. From earliest times attempts have been made to interpret the saying acceptably: e.g. Matthew (12:31f.) already expanded the saying and gave his own interpretation of it which is different from Mark's. But we are here concerned only with what Mark made of it or with what we are to make of the form in which he reported it.

3:29 *Whoever blasphemes against the Holy Spirit never has forgiveness, but is guilty of an eternal sin* The Greek word for 'eternal' refers to the age to come. The background of this saying was the rabbinic teaching that those who commit certain heinous sins have no part in the age to come. So Jesus may here be saying, 'whatever the rabbis teach about the comparative heinousness of sins, there is in truth only one absolutely heinous sin, namely blasphemy against the Holy Spirit, i.e. ascribing what is manifestly the work of God's Spirit to the devil.' To call good evil leads to a complete blunting of moral sensibility. The impossibility of this sin's being forgiven is due not to God's unwillingness to forgive, but to the sinner's incapacity to receive forgiveness, since he has made himself incapable of repenting.

3:30 This verse is an editorial comment, recalling v. 22.

31 And his mother and his brothers came; and standing outside they sent to him and called him. 32 And a crowd was sitting about him; and they said to him, 'Your mother and your brothers are outside, asking for you.'

33 And he replied, 'Who are my mother and my brothers?' 34 And looking around on those who sat about him, he said, 'Here are my mother and my brothers! 35 Whoever does the will of God is my brother, and sister, and mother.'

The point of this anecdote is clearly the saying of Jesus in v. 35: it is what is technically known as 'a pronouncement story'. It does not imply that Jesus thought lightly of family ties, but rather that obedience to the will of God or the calling to serve God was so imperative as to override this closest of human bonds and obligations. The saying must have been of great importance for the early Christians, as it has been in later times for those who have answered the call to the religious life or to missionary work overseas. The fact that Joseph is not mentioned may mean that he was dead.

3:31 *His brothers* There have been three theories about who they were, named after the proponents thereof in the fourth century A.D. (i) *The Helvidian view.* Helvidius said that they were sons of Joseph and Mary, i.e. younger brothers of Jesus. Tertullian held this view. (ii) *The Epiphanian view.* Epiphanius said that they were sons of Joseph by a former marriage, i.e. step-brothers of Jesus. (iii) *The Hieronymian view.* Named after Jerome, this said that they were cousins of Jesus. The later belief in the perpetual virginity of Mary has inevitably influenced opinion on the subject. While the Helvidian view is the most natural interpretation of the word 'brothers', the other views might help to explain the reported attitude of the brethren to Jesus during his ministry. *Standing outside* could mean outside the house or on the edge of the crowd.

3:35 The bond that unites the family of God is obedience to his will.

4:1 Again he began to teach beside the sea. And a very large crowd gathered about him, so that he got into a boat and sat in it on the sea; and the whole crowd was beside the sea on the land. 2 And he taught them many things in parables, and in his teaching he said to them: 3 'Listen! A sower went out to sow. 4 And as he sowed, some seed fell along the path, and the birds came and devoured it. 5 Other seed fell on rocky ground, where it had not much soil, and immediately it sprang up, since it had no depth of soil; 6 and when the sun rose it was scorched, and since it had no root it withered away. 7 Other seed fell among thorns and the thorns grew up and choked it, and it yielded no grain. 8 And other seeds fell into good soil and brought forth grain, growing up and increasing and yielding thirtyfold and sixtyfold and a hundredfold.' 9 And he said, 'He who has ears to hear, let him hear.'

In this chapter for the first time Mark gives some account of the content of the teaching of Jesus, but it is a limited account. He only narrates some parables and seeks to explain why Jesus taught in parables. Children used to be told that a parable is 'an earthly story with a heavenly meaning', but the truth of the matter is much more complicated than that.

The word *parable* is derived from the Greek word *parabolé* which means putting things side by side as in a comparison. In the New Testament it is used to translate a wide-ranging Hebrew word. It covers not only stories but proverbial sayings and illustrations of various kinds (cp. note on 3:23). As regards stories, like the rabbis Jesus evidently told them often in order to drive home or get across his teaching. Mark however is going to say in vv. 11f. that their purpose was to conceal the truth. How is this to be explained?

Every teacher or preacher, who uses stories to clarify a point, knows that pictures stick in the memory when abstract teaching is forgotten and that stories are easily remembered when the point they were intended to illustrate has been forgotten. They are remembered and repeated, that is to say, apart from their context. This happened to many of the stories which Jesus told and that is why they are commonly introduced with the quite general formula, 'The kingdom of God is like . . .' When separated from their original context and the particular point they were meant to illustrate, they could be interpreted in various ways, for one story may be used on different occasions to illustrate different points. Alternatively, when the point of a story has been lost, it may come to be regarded as a puzzle or enigma which only initiates or the enlightened can penetrate, and hence as designed to conceal the truth from others. Or again, stories can be turned into allegories. Whereas a normal parabolic story originally had only one point, however many details it contained, in an allegory every detail is regarded as symbolic of something or other. All these things happened to the stories told by Jesus.

4:1f. These verses provide a picturesque setting which however seems to be disregarded in v. 10. Matthew Henry engagingly comments: 'That inland sea of Tiberias having no tide, there was no ebbing and flowing of the waters to disturb them. Methinks Christ's carrying his doctrine into a ship, and preaching it thence, was a presage of his sending the gospel to the isles of the Gentiles, and the shipping off of the kingdom of God (that rich cargo) from the Jewish nation, to be sent to a people that would bring forth more of the fruits of it.'

4:3-8 This is generally known as 'the parable of the sower' but it would more aptly be described as 'the parable of the soils'. The picture of a sower scattering seed was often used in antiquity for the teacher (e.g. see 2 Esdras 9:31, 33). In Palestine sowing precedes ploughing; so here seed is deliberately sown on the hard ground which will be ploughed afterwards. *Rocky ground* means places where the soil is thin and the rock is near the surface. We cannot be sure what was the point of the parable in its original context. It may have been to encourage the disciples with the thought that in their preaching, while they would encounter many failures and obstacles, the outcome would be abundantly worthwhile; or Jesus may have been speaking of his own ministry, which despite opposition and lack of response, would produce a rich harvest, and by the time the gospel was written it had done that. Or the story may have simply aimed at enforcing the duty of being a good listener.

4:9 *He who has ears, let him hear.* 'If a man has ears, let him use them' (Ba). It is a summons to attentive hearing.

10 And when he was alone, those who were about him with the twelve asked him concerning the parables. 11 And he said to them, 'To you has been given the secret of the kingdom of God, but for those outside everything is in parables; 12 so that they may indeed see but not perceive, and may indeed hear but not understand; lest they should turn again, and be forgiven.' 13 And he said to them, 'Do you not understand this parable? How then will you understand all the parables? 14 The sower sows the word. 15 And these are the ones along the path, where the word is sown; when they hear, Satan immediately comes and takes away the word which is sown in them. 16 And these in like manner are the ones sown upon rocky ground, who, when they hear the word, immediately receive it with joy; 17 and they have no root in themselves, but endure for a while; then, when tribulation or persecution arises on account of the word, immediately they fall away. 18 And others are the ones sown among thorns; they are those who hear the word, 19 but the cares of the world, and the delight in riches, and the desire for other things, enter in and choke the word, and it proves unfruitful. 20 But those that were sown upon the good soil are the ones who hear the word and accept it and bear fruit, thirtyfold and sixtyfold and a hundredfold.'

4:10 Verses 11f. were apparently a separate saying

that was inserted here because it had to do with parables. It breaks the connection between 10 and 13 and is artificially combined with them. In 10 *parables* should be singular – *the parable* as in A.V.: it was made a plural to suit 11f. In 12 the word 'parables' probably signified not parabolic stories, but aphorisms, proverbial and enigmatic sayings. It may be that it was the later Christian community that made this enquiry about parables.

4:11f. This saying reflects the idea (derived from the Old Testament and also elaborated in Romans chapters 9-11) that the Lord taught in such a way as to conceal the truth from those hearers who were not called or elected to receive and respond to it. Parables could have the effect of hardening unbelievers even if that were not their direct intention. The scriptural quotation is a paraphrase of Isaiah 6:9f. It is also possible that for readers of the gospel this saying may have been taken to imply that Christianity was 'a mystery religion' like those that were familiar in the Hellenistic world. (The word translated *secret* in R.S.V. is *musterion*, i.e. mystery, as in A.V. and R.V.)

Only those who were initiated could understand the secret or esoteric doctrine which was hidden from outsiders. What later came to be known as *disciplina arcani* (discipline of the secret), according to which some theological doctrines and religious practices were concealed from catechumens and pagans, bears a resemblance to this, as does also the idea (dear to the nineteenth-century Tractarians) about 'reserve in communicating religious knowledge'. Has the concept of 'mystery' been too much jettisoned by modern Christianity?

Perhaps the best translation of 11f. is that of J. Jeremias: 'To you God has given the secret of the kingdom of God; but to those who are without everything is obscure, in order that they (as it is written) may "see and yet not see, may hear and yet not understand, unless they turn and God will forgive them".' Cp. 'that they may look and look but not see, and listen and listen but not understand' (We).

4:13-20 This is an allegorical interpretation of the parable, presumably the work of an early Christian preacher, who took the parable as a text for a sermon. Maybe it was Mark himself. It reflects the experience of the Church and the different reactions to the apostolic preaching. The interpretation is somewhat confused. The hearers are identified with the seed and not, as we should expect, with the soils. The parable is interpreted as 'a warning and encouragement to Christians in conditions of persecution and worldly temptation' (N), which is suitable for the time when the gospel was composed but not for the situation depicted in 1f.

21 And he said to them, 'Is a lamp brought in to be put under a bushel, or under a bed, and not on a stand? 22 For there is nothing hid, except to be made manifest; nor is anything secret, except to come to light. 23 If any man has ears to hear, let him hear'. 24 And he said to them, 'Take heed what you hear; the measure you give will be the measure you get, and still more will be given you. 25 For to him who has will more be given; and from him who has not, even what he has will be taken away.'

This is a string of five or six detached parabolic sayings, which will have been in circulation apart from their original context. Mark seems to have regarded them as meaning that while the mystery of the kingdom (the messianic secret, etc.) was intended to be concealed during the ministry of Jesus, this was not his ultimate purpose. After the resurrection the gospel was to be fully disclosed and proclaimed and this was to be the responsibility of the disciples.

4:21f. *A lamp* The A.V.'s *candle* and *candle-stick* are incorrect since candles were not used in Palestine at that time. The point is that if God hides anything, it is with the purpose of finally revealing it. It is the *raison d'être* of a lamp to give light. So this saying is a mitigation of 11f.

'The church must never retreat into a ghetto or become a petty sect. She must be a sign to God in the world' (Sch).

4:23 The repetition of these words stresses the importance of what is being said.

4:24 *Take heed what you hear* . . . You will grow in understanding in so far as you attend carefully to what you have already received.

4:25 *For to him who has will more be given* . . . 'A popular proverb, coined perhaps by some cynical observer of oriental society, who had noticed how presents were given to rich men, while the poor man, who had nothing, was fleeced to the last farthing' (R). This applies to mental and spiritual life also. If a man has a well-stored mind, he will be continually adding to that store, whereas small knowledge tends to decrease.

26 And he said, 'The Kingdom of God is as if a man should scatter seed upon the ground, 27 and should sleep and rise night and day, and the seed should sprout and grow, he knows not how. 28 The earth produces of itself, first the blade, then the ear, then the full grain in the ear. 29 But when the grain is ripe, at once he puts in the sickle, because the harvest has come.'

This parable of the seed growing secretly or of the fruit-bearing earth is the only one in Mark that was not reproduced by Matthew and Luke. Did they jib at the suggestion that the kingdom comes *of itself*, i.e. automatically? We don't know the circumstances in which the parable was originally spoken or what it was intended to illustrate. Various suggestions have been made about its meaning of which the more plausible are: (i) it could be affirming the certainty that God's kingdom would come once the seed had been sown, whatever the immediate appearances; (ii) it is affirming that it is God who produces the harvest, therefore the disciples, like the farmer, should put their trust in him; (iii) it may be a parable of contrast:

'as seed time is followed in due time by harvest, so will
the present hiddenness and ambiguousness of the kingdom
of God be succeeded by its glorious manifestation' (Cr).
The last is the most likely, as the next parable will be
making the same point.

4:27 *Night and day* in accordance with Jewish usage,
not 'day and night'.

4:29 There is an echo of Joel 3:13 in this verse.

30 And he said, 'With what can we compare the
kingdom of God, or what parable shall we use for it?
31 It is like a grain of mustard seed, which, when sown
upon the ground, is the smallest of all the seeds on earth;
32 yet when it is sown it grows up and becomes the
greatest of all shrubs, and puts forth large branches, so
that the birds of the air can make nests in its shade.'

The point of the parable of the mustard seed is not that
the kingdom of God gradually grows and evolves in the
course of history (as nineteenth-century believers in evolu-
tion and progress used to suppose), but the contrast between
the smallness of the seed and what comes of it. The kingdom of God was almost imperceptible during the ministry
of Jesus, in sharp contrast to the way in which it will be
gloriously manifested at its future consummation.

4:31 *The smallest of all the seeds on earth* It was
not so in fact, but it may have been proverbially so in
Palestine.

4:32 *The greatest of all shrubs* It attains a height of
eight to twelve feet by the lake of Gennesaret, and small
birds are said to alight upon its stalks and pluck the seeds,
though not to build their nests in it. *So that the birds of
the air can make nests in its shade* For Mark this may have
meant that as a result of the preaching of the gospel
members of all nations will be able to find a place in the
church.

33 With many such parables he spoke the word to

them, as they were able to hear it; 34 he did not speak
to them without a parable, but privately to his own disciples he explained everything.

A summary statement about parabolic teaching.

4:33 *As they were able to hear it* This contradicts the
theory about the use of parables in 12f.

4:34 *He did not speak to them without a parable* This
is surely an exaggeration.

35 On that day, when evening had come, he said to
them, 'Let us go across to the other side.' 36 And
leaving the crowd, they took him with them, in the boat,
just as he was. And other boats were with him. 37 And
a great storm of wind arose, and the waves beat into the
boat, so that the boat was already filling. 38 But he was
in the stern, asleep on the cushion; and they woke him
and said to him, 'Teacher, do you not care if we perish?'
39 And he awoke and rebuked the wind, and said to the
sea, 'Peace! Be still!' And the wind ceased, and there
was a great calm. 40 He said to them, 'Why are you
afraid? Have you no faith?' 41 And they were filled
with awe, and said to one another, 'Who then is this,
that even wind and sea obey him?'

This story of the stilling of the storm was manifestly
much valued in the early Church. Matthew and Luke tell
it with variations; see also John chapter 6. It brought
assurance that, however indifferent God might seem to be
to his people when attacked by storms of persecution and
hostility, he was not really so. Mark's first readers, surrounded by the stormy atmosphere of Nero's Rome, were
having a rough time when he composed his gospel, so that
the story would particularly speak to their condition. Sudden storms were (and are) liable to blow up on the lake
and to subside as suddenly. This story may have been
influenced by some verses in the Psalms: see 93:3f.;
69:1f., 14f.; 107:23-29.

4:36 *They took him with them . . . just as he was*
'Without any cloak to throw over him, which he ought
to have had to keep him warm, when he went to sea at
night, especially after preaching' (H). *And other boats
were with him* This seems to be the recollection of an eyewitness, since the 'other boats' serve no purpose in the
story.

4:38 *He was in the stern, asleep on the cushion* Some
think that this was the wooden or leather seat for the
steersman; others a cushion kept for the seat of honour in
the stern. Note the contrast between the complete confidence of Jesus in the providence of God and the frightened and faithless disciples.

4:39 *Peace! Be still!* words addressed to the demonic
powers who were thought to be the cause of such storms.
So this is a case of exorcism, rather than a 'nature miracle'. *There was a great calm* 'of the sea; which, in other
circumstances, would have continued in a troubled state
even after the wind had lulled' (Be).

4:40 Mark's readers may have seen, as we may, the
boat and its passengers as representing the Church and
themselves, and may have taken to themselves the rebuke,
Have you no faith? as well as the encouragement provided by the outcome.

4:41 *Who then is this?* For Mark the answer is: The
Messiah, the Son of God. He implies that this truth is beginning to dawn in the minds of the disciples.

5:1 They came to the other side of the sea, to the
country of the Gerasenes. 2 And when he had come
out of the boat there met him out of the tombs a man
with an unclean spirit, 3 who lived among the tombs;
and no one could bind him any more, even with chains;
4 for he had often been bound with fetters and chains,
but the chains he wrenched apart, and the fetters he
broke in pieces; and no one had the strength to subdue
him. 5 Night and day among the tombs and on the
mountains he was always crying out, and bruising him-

self with stones. 6 And when he saw Jesus from afar, he ran and worshipped him; 7 and crying out with a loud voice, he said, 'What have you to do with me, Jesus, Son of the Most High God? I adjure you by God, do not torment me.' 8 For he had said to him, 'Come out of the man, you unclean spirit!' 9 And Jesus asked him, 'What is your name?' He replied, 'My name is Legion; for we are many.' 10 And he begged him eagerly not to send them out of the country. 11 Now a great herd of swine was feeding there on the hillside; 12 and they begged him, 'Send us to the swine, let us enter them.' 13 So he gave them leave. And the unclean spirits came out, and entered the swine; and the herd, numbering about two thousand, rushed down the steep bank into the sea, and were drowned in the sea. 14 The herdsmen fled, and told it in the city and in the country. And people came to see what it was that had happened. 15 And they came to Jesus, and saw the demoniac sitting there, clothed and in his right mind, the man who had had the legion; and they were afraid. 16 And those who had seen it told what had happened to the demoniac and to the swine. 17 And they began to beg Jesus to depart from their neighbourhood. 18 And as he was getting into the boat, the man who had been possessed with demons begged him that he might go with them. 19 But he refused, and said to him, 'Go home to your friends, and tell them how much the Lord has done for you, and how he has had mercy on you.' 20 And he went away and began to proclaim in the Decapolis how much Jesus had done for him; and all men marvelled.

This story of the Gerasene demoniac has puzzled or put off many people. It is said, for instance, that T. H. Huxley regarded it as a decisive objection to accepting the claims of Christ, since no good man would treat dumb animals as Jesus is here represented as doing. A likely explanation is that an authentic story about Jesus restoring a demented man to sanity (an outstanding instance of the healing power of God at work) has here been combined with, or elaborated by, a colourful popular folk tale which originally had nothing to do with Jesus.

5:1 *Gerasenes* There is much confusion and uncertainty about this name, and there are different readings in different manuscripts, *Gergesenes* and *Gadarenes* occurring as well as *Gerasenes*, though it seems that the last is what Mark wrote. Gerasa was thirty miles or more from the lake, and so is ruled out. Gadara was six miles from the shore, which makes it a very improbable location. Gergesa has not been identified, but the ruins of a small town named Kersa, on the east side of the lake, have been unearthed. 'The Gadarene swine,' etc. have become proverbial – J. L. Garvin once accused the pacifist George Lansbury of being ready for 'the Gadarene gallop' – but the expression is certainly a misnomer.

5:3 *Who lived among the tombs* Demons were popularly supposed to haunt cemeteries. In Palestine tombs were often caves: cp. Hebrews 11:38, 'in dens and caves of the earth'. For Jews tombs were unclean, but this man may have been a pagan. That part of the country was semipagan, as is shown by the presence of swine, which Jews were forbidden to keep. The story may have been influenced by Isaiah 65:4f.

5:4 *Bound with fetters and chains* This illustrates the cruel way in which the mad used to be treated, though it was done no doubt to protect other people.

5:5 *He was always crying out, and bruising himself with stones* 'He shrieked and gashed himself with stones' (M).

5:6 *He ran and worshipped him* 'he ran and flung himself down before him' (NEB). 'A specimen and foretaste of the Lordship of Christ' (Be). In Mark's view he at once recognized the supernatural character of Jesus, since the demons had supernatural knowledge, as appears in v. 7.

5:9 *What is your name?* The ancients attached much importance to knowing the name of one's adversary, e.g. see Genesis 32:27, 29, and it was thought that an exorcist gained power over a demon by knowing its name. *My name is Legion; for we are many* A legion normally consisted of 6000 men. 'In applying this name to himself the possessed man appealed to Christ's pity. It meant that he felt himself to be a mere congeries of unco-ordinated impulses and evil forces – lacking a moral unity of will, and so not one but an aggregate of many' (Bartlett). 'The man was like an image of heathendom', said Bishop Christopher Wordsworth. 'The gentile world was then beleaguered by many legions of evil spirits; it could not be bound by any laws, it tore them asunder; Christ came from heaven to deliver it from these evil spirits and to cast them out; so that being clothed in the robe of faith and in its right mind, it might come to sit at his feet. It came and sat like a scholar at the feet of the Divine Teacher.' Can it not also be said that the man is an image of our world to-day?

5:10 *Not to send them out of the country* It was believed that demons were associated with particular localities.

5:13 *The unclean spirits came out, and entered the swine; and the herd . . . rushed down* It has been suggested that the shrieks and gestures of the man so frightened the swine that they stampeded, and that Jesus in effect said, 'See, there go your demons' – a skilful piece of psychological suggestion, i.e. Jesus took advantage of a lamentable natural calamity to clinch a cure. But isn't this attempted rationalization of the story far-fetched? Better with Branscomb to say: 'As it stands . . . the narrative is a good story which should not be spoiled.'

5:15 *And they were afraid*. This is the awe felt by those who experience the supernatural.

5:17 *And they began to beg Jesus to depart* 'While the people had been deeply impressed by the sight of the restored man, the tale of what had happened to the swine convinced them that Jesus was a public danger' (T). What might happen next? They wanted a quiet, undisturbed life. Don't we all?

5:19 *Go home to your friends, and tell them* This appears to be inconsistent with the repeated injunctions to secrecy in Mark. Some explain it by saying that there was no question of the man's revealing the messiahship of Jesus. He is told only to tell his friends how much God had done for him. What Jesus said to him may have meant: 'Keep it in the family circle.'

5:20 However, the man disobeys Jesus's injunction *Decapolis* (=ten cities) This was a league of cities east of Jordan which enjoyed some independence and was mainly gentile.

21 And when Jesus had crossed again in the boat to the other side, a great crowd gathered about him; and he was beside the sea. 22 Then came one of the rulers of the synagogue, Jairus by name; and seeing him, he fell at his feet, 23 and besought him, saying, 'My little daughter is at the point of death. Come and lay your hands on her, so that she may be made well and live.' 24 And he went with him. And a great crowd followed him and thronged about him. 25 And there was a woman who had had a flow of blood for twelve years, 26 and who had suffered much under many physicians, and had spent all that she had, and was no better but rather grew worse. 27 She had heard the reports about Jesus and came up behind him in the crowd and touched his garment. 28 For she said, 'If I touch even his garment, I shall be made well.' 29 And immediately the haemorrhage ceased; and she felt in her body that she was healed of her disease. 30 And Jesus, perceiving in himself that power had gone forth from him, immediately turned about in the crowd, and said, 'Who touched my garments?' 31 And his disciples said to him, 'You see the crowd pressing around you, and yet you say, "Who touched me?"' 32 And he looked around to see who had done it. 33 But the woman, knowing what had been done to her, came in fear and trembling and fell down before him, and told him the whole truth. 34 And he said

to her, 'Daughter, your faith has made you well; go in peace, and be healed of your disease.' 35 While he was still speaking, there came from the ruler's house some who said, 'Your daughter is dead. Why trouble the Teacher any further?'. 36 But ignoring what they said, Jesus said to the ruler of the synagogue, 'Do not fear, only believe.' 37 And he allowed no one to follow him except Peter and James and John the brother of James. 38 When they came to the house of the ruler of the synagogue, he saw a tumult, and people weeping and wailing loudly. 39 And when he had entered, he said to them, 'Why do you make a tumult and weep? The child is not dead but sleeping.' 40 And they laughed at him. But he put them all outside, and took the child's father and mother and those who were with him, and went in where the child was. 41 Taking her by the hand he said to her, '*Talitha cumi*'; which means; 'Little girl, I say to you, arise.' 42 And immediately the girl got up and walked (she was twelve years of age) and they were immediately overcome with amazement. 43 And he strictly charged them that no one should know this, and told them to give her something to eat.

5:21 *Jesus crossed . . . to the other side* i.e. to the west side of the lake, to the neighbourhood of Capernaum. *A great crowd gathered about him* 'swarmed round him'.

5:22 *One of the rulers of the synagogue* 'one of the Wardens of the synagogue' (We): a lay official responsible for the oversight of the building and its services – an important person in the locality. *Jairus by name* The textual evidence makes it probable that the name was not given by Mark, but was supplied later. Early Christian writers were fond of naming anonymous individuals in the gospel stories.

5:23 *So that she may be made well* The same Greek word can mean 'heal' or 'save' or both.

5:25 *A woman who had had a flow of blood* i.e. a haemorrhage. 'The nature of the disorder made her reluctant to mention it.' (Sc).

5:26 *Who had suffered much under many physicians*
Deprecation of the medical profession was common in
ancient literature. It was a vexatious custom in the east to
call in as many physicians as possible, with the consequence
that their prescriptions clashed, cost much money, and
made the malady worse.

5:28 It was a popular belief that a supernatural power
of healing could, as it were, be tapped by touching the
clothes of holy men.

5:29 *She felt in her body that she was healed of her
disease* on which M. Henry comments: 'Note, those whom
Christ heals of the disease of sin, that bloody issue, cannot
but experience in themselves an universal change for the
better.'

5:30 *Who touched my garments?* 'Being desirous to see
his patient, he asked, not in displeasure as one affronted,
but in tenderness as one concerned' (H).

5:32 *And he looked around to see who had done it*
A.V. and R.V. more correctly translate 'to see her who had
done this thing', implying that he knew in advance that it
was a woman, or it may be that Mark is simply writing
from his own standpoint.

5:33 *The woman . . . came in fear and trembling* Why?
Was she embarrassed by having become the centre of
attention? Or is it because she was aware of the miracle
that had been done for her? Or was she afraid that Jesus
might be angry with her? 'As the touch of persons thus
diseased communicated ceremonial pollution, this perhaps increased her fears' (Sc).

5:34 *Your faith has made you well* i.e. her trust in the
power of God to heal, which was at work in Jesus. 'The
consistent New Testament view of faith is that it derives
its content and virtue from the object in which it rests'
(T).

5:35 *Your daughter is dead. Why trouble the Teacher
any further?* This implies that power to raise the dead
had not yet been attributed to Jesus.

5:36 *But ignoring what they said* The word translated 'ignoring' can mean either 'overhear' (so N.E.B.) or 'pay no heed to'. Either makes good sense here.

5.38 *People weeping and wailing loudly* These may have been professional mourners. 'Them that chanted the funeral dirge' (Be).

5:39 *The child is not dead but sleeping* Some have thought that Jesus was saying, 'She is in a coma'. But this is very unlikely, although it would make it easier for modern people to credit the story. Jesus probably meant that though the child was indeed dead, yet, as he was going to restore her to life, her death would be no more lasting than sleep. At the same time 'for believing readers, these words are a revelation: death is only sleep, in the light of faith, from which there is an awakening through the power of God' (Sch).

5:40 *They laughed at him* They took his words about her in a literal sense, whereas they knew she was really dead.

5:41 *Talitha cumi* Aramaic for *Little girl, I say to you, arise* Origen remarked that it was well known that spells and incantations lost their power if translated into a foreign language. It is possible that Mark translates the words here to correct such a superstitious notion.

5.43 *And told them to give her something to eat* T. R. Glover noted that this clause was characteristic of our Lord's sense of the sober realities of a situation. 'He reminded a too happy father that his little girl would be the better for food.'

This is the climax of the present series of miracles or signs in Mark's gospel. This one (like the widow's son at Nain and Lazarus at Bethany) was a case of resuscitation to a further spell of mortal life, not of resurrection to eternal life as in the case of Christ himself. It is idle to enquire how these stories of resuscitation are to be explained, since we do not have anything like sufficient data for the purpose. It is better to regard them as signal illustrations of the truth that Christ came that men might have

life and have it abundantly (John 10:10) and that the final
outcome of his ministry on earth was to be life and not
death.

6:1 He went away from there and came to his own
country; and his disciples followed him. 2 And on the
sabbath he began to teach in the synagogue; and many
who heard him were astonished, saying, 'Where did this
man get all this? What is the wisdom given to him?
What mighty works are wrought by his hands! 3 Is
not this the carpenter, the son of Mary and brother of
James and Joses and Judas and Simon, and are not his
sisters here with us?' And they took offence at him. 4
And Jesus said to them, 'A prophet is not without
honour, except in his own country, and among his own
kin, and in his own house.' 5 And he could do no mighty
work there, except that he laid his hands upon a few
sick people and healed them. 6 And he marvelled because of their unbelief.

Some commentators consider that a new section of the
gospel opens here, others place a division at 6:14, but
neither here nor there is there any evident break with what
has preceded. Mark continued to string together the separate stories or units that were at his disposal in whatever
struck him as a suitable order. We saw that at 3:6 Jesus
appeared to break with the synagogue, but here he makes
one last return to it and is rejected again. This fore-
shadows his final rejection by his people. 'The Nazarenes
. . . are typical of those who "see and do not perceive,
hear and do not understand"' (Sch).

6:1 *And came to his own country* The word translated
'country' can equally well mean 'his native town', i.e.
Nazareth. Mark has no reference to Bethlehem as Jesus's
birthplace.

6:2 *Many who heard him* could also mean 'all who
were present'.

6:3 *Is not this the carpenter, the son of Mary?* 'He's

only the carpenter, Mary's son' (P). This is probably correct, though there is an alternative reading: 'Is not this the son of the carpenter?' It was insulting to refer to someone as the son of his mother: see Judges 11:1. 'Carpenter' can equally well be translated 'builder' or 'joiner' or 'stonemason'. 'Jewish fathers were bound to teach their children some trade' (Sc). For the brothers of Jesus, see note on 3:31. *And they took offence at him* 'They were shocked and resentful that someone they knew so well should speak and act like that' (Ba).

6:4 *A prophet is not without honour* This may have been a proverbial saying. It occurs in a different context in John 4:43. There is an interesting apocryphal variant of it: 'A prophet is not acceptable in his own country, nor doth a physician do cures upon them that know him.' 'If it be true that a prophet is not received in his own country, it is equally true that he is not received in his own age' (B. F. Westcott).

6:5 *He could do no mighty work there* because it was morally impossible in the face of unbelief. Matthew (13:58) modified the statement, considering it to be derogatory to our Lord. For the same reason the second half of this verse may have been added as a gloss.

6:6 *He marvelled because of their unbelief* 'Note', says M. Henry, 'the unbelief of those that enjoy the means of grace, is a most amazing thing.'

6b And he went about among the villages teaching. 7 And he called to him the twelve, and began to send them out two by two, and gave them authority over the unclean spirits. 8 He charged them to take nothing for their journey except a staff; no bread, no bag, no money in their belts; 9 but to wear sandals and not to put on two tunics. 10 And he said to them, 'Where you enter a house, stay there until you leave the place. 11 And if any place will not receive you and they refuse to hear you, when you leave, shake off the dust that is on your feet for a testimony against them.' 12 So they went out and preached that men should repent. 13 And they cast out many demons, and anointed with oil many that were sick and healed them.

6:6b *He went about among the villages* He made a tour round the villages. As is usual with Mark, we are told that Jesus taught, but not what he was teaching.

6:7 *He . . . began to send them out* 'For the evangelist and his readers, this mission of the disciples becomes a prototype of the mission which is imposed on, and entrusted to, the Church' (Sch). A set of instructions for missionaries was evidently in circulation in the early Church. See Matthew 10; Luke 9:1-5; 10:1-16. Mark here seems to be using an abridged form of it, and to be reading back into the time of Jesus a mission and missionary instructions that belong to the time when the apostles set out on evangelistic tours in Palestine. The setting here is extremely vague: as has been said, it 'hangs in the air'. On the other hand, Albert Schweitzer held that this mission of the disciples was an urgent, last-minute appeal of Jesus to his nation, and others have thought it played a more important part in the Lord's ministry than Mark realized or enables us to understand. The story is not intrinsically unlikely since similar missionary activity was a familiar feature of the Hellenistic world. *Two by two* Travelling in pairs was a Jewish custom which was followed by the Christians. 'They went two and two . . . that they might be company for one another when they were among strangers, and might strengthen the hands and encourage the hearts of one another; might help one another if anything should be amiss, and keep one another in countenance' (H). Doesn't this still apply? *Gave them authority over the unclean spirits* See 3:15. There is plenty of evidence in the New Testament that the apostles continued this aspect of the ministry of Jesus.

6:8 *He charged them to take nothing for their journey* These instructions vary in the different gospels. No doubt account was taken of the fact that what was feasible in

Palestine was not so elsewhere. These are not to be regarded, nor were they from the first regarded, as timeless laws for missionary activity, though in many respects they have an enduring point, e.g. travelling light and not fussing about superfluous accessories. 'The young Church understood that the instructions of Jesus which were suited to that time do not remain literally obligatory, as is shown by the divergence in Matthew and Luke. What counts is the spirit of apostolic simplicity' (Sch). What does 'the spirit of apostolic simplicity' require of Christians today? *No bag* – presumably a collecting bag, not a bag for provisions. *No money in their belts* It was usual to carry small change in one's girdle. We should say 'no money in their pockets'.

6:10 *When you enter a house, stay there* 'Make it your home till you leave that place' (We). When they had accepted hospitality in a modest house, they were not to move on if they were offered more commodious lodging. The second-century writing known as the *Didache* lays it down that a travelling missionary should not expect to stay for more than two or three days. If he stays longer he should work for his keep.

6:11 *When you leave, shake off the dust* When pious Jews re-entered the Holy Land after travelling abroad they were carefully to remove the dust of heathen territory from their feet and clothing, so that the action prescribed here would be equivalent to declaring the place pagan. The action would be calculated to make the inhabitants think again. *A testimony against them* N.E.B. has 'as a warning to them'. Barclay has 'to make them see the seriousness of what they have done'.

6:12f. These verses, like 7, were composed by Mark to provide a framework of narrative for the missionary charge. *Anointed with oil* cp. James 5:10. This was a common practice in the east: oil was used not only because of its medicinal properties but also because of a certain sacramental efficacy. Thus the ecclesiastical sacrament of holy unction has its roots in the New Testament. What importance ought we to attach to it today?

14 King Herod heard of it; for Jesus's name had become known. Some said, 'John the baptizer has been raised from the dead; that is why these powers are at work in him.' 15 But others said, 'It is Elijah.' And others said, 'It is a prophet, like one of the prophets of old.' 16 But when Herod heard of it he said, 'John, whom I beheaded, has been raised.'

Mark may have inserted here this account of Herod's impression of Jesus and of the death of John, to fill in the time before the disciples returned from their mission.

6:14 *King Herod heard of it* This was Herod Antipas, son of Herod the Great. Actually he was not a king, but the tetrarch of Galilee and Perea. His ambition to be a king led eventually to his downfall. He was banished by the Emperor Caligula in A.D. 39. Herod presumably had heard reports about Jesus and/or the opinions about him that were current.

6:15 *Others said, 'It is Elijah'* see note on 1:5ff. *Like one of the prophets of old* The voice of prophecy had been silent for a long time.

6:16 *John, whom I beheaded* Herod says, 'It is John the baptizer all over again.' Or does he mean that Jesus is really John come to life again?

17 For Herod had sent and seized John, and bound him in prison for the sake of Herodias, his brother Philip's wife; because he had married her. 18 For John said to Herod, 'It is not lawful for you to have your brother's wife.' 19 And Herodias had a grudge against him, and wanted to kill him. But she could not, 20 for Herod feared John, knowing that he was a righteous and holy man, and kept him safe. When he heard him, he was much perplexed; and yet he heard him gladly. 21

But an opportunity came when Herod on his birthday gave a banquet for his courtiers and officers and the leading men of Galilee. 22 For when Herodias's daughter came in and danced, she pleased Herod and his guests, and the king said to the girl, 'Ask me for whatever you wish, and I will grant it.' 23 And he vowed to her, 'Whatever you ask me, I will give you, even half of my kingdom.' 24 And she went out, and said to her mother, 'What shall I ask?' And she said, 'The head of John the baptizer.' 25 And she came in immediately with haste to the king, and asked, saying, 'I want you to give me at once the head of John the Baptist on a platter.' 26 And the king was exceedingly sorry; but because of his oaths and his guests he did not want to break his word to her. 27 And immediately the king sent a soldier of the guard and gave orders to bring his head. He went and beheaded him in the prison, 28 and brought his head on a platter, and gave it to the girl; and the girl gave it to her mother. 29 When his disciples heard of it, they came and took his body, and laid it in a tomb.

The Jewish historian Josephus gives a different account of the death of John, and ascribes it to political motives on Herod's part. Of the story in Mark, Rawlinson well said that it is 'an account, written with a certain amount of literary freedom, of what was being darkly whispered in the bazaars or market places of Palestine at the time'.

6:17 *Herodias, his brother Philip's wife* Mark is confused about the names, as he well might be, considering the complicated relationships of the Herod family. Herodias was not Philip's wife, but the wife of another son of Herod the Great.

6:18 *It is not lawful for you to have your brother's wife* See Leviticus 18:16; 20:21.

6:20 *Kept him safe* According to Josephus, John was imprisoned at Machaerus which was a frontier fortress on the Dead Sea and also a palace.

6:23 *I will give you, even half of my kingdom* The story has probably been influenced by the book of Esther (see 5:1-3). A king tricked by his own oath is a popular theme in stories of this kind.

6:28 *And brought his head on a platter* – as though it were one of the courses at the banquet.

6:29 *They . . . took his body, and laid it in a tomb* The man of God finds peace at last.

30 The apostles returned to Jesus, and told him all that they had done and taught. 31 And he said to them, 'Come away by yourselves to a lonely place, and rest a while.' For many were coming and going, and they had no leisure even to eat. 32 And they went away in the boat to a lonely place by themselves. 33 Now many saw them going, and knew them, and they ran there on foot from all the towns, and got there ahead of them. 34 As he went ashore he saw a great throng, and he had compassion on them, because they were like sheep without a shepherd; and he began to teach them many things. 35 And when it grew late, his disciples came to him and said, 'This is a lonely place, and the hour is now late; 36 send them away, to go into the country and villages round about and buy themselves something to eat.' 37 But he answered them, 'You give them something to eat.' And they said to him, 'Shall we go and buy them two hundred denarii worth of bread, and give it to them to eat?' 38 And he said to them, 'How many loaves have you? Go and see.' And when they had found out, they said, 'Five, and two fish.' 39 Then he commanded them all to sit down by companies upon the green grass. 40 So they sat down in groups, by hundreds and by fifties. 41 And taking the five loaves and two fish he looked up to heaven, and blessed, and broke the loaves, and gave them to the disciples to set them before the people, and he divided the two fish among them all. 42 And they all ate, and were satisfied. 43 And they took up twelve baskets full of broken pieces and

of the fish. 44 And those who ate the loaves were five thousand men.

6:30 *The apostles returned to Jesus, and told him all that they had done and taught* This is the only place where Mark calls the disciples 'apostles', and he probably uses it in its literal sense of 'missionaries', those who are sent, rather than in the restricted sense it acquired later. On this verse M. Henry comments: 'Ministers are accountable both for what they do, and for what they teach . . . Let them not either do any thing, or teach any thing, but what they are willing should be related and repeated to the Lord Jesus.' A searching test.

6:31 *Come away by yourselves to a lonely place* i.e. to the desert or wilderness where the Israelites had of old received many evidences of God's care for them, including the manna. *They had no leisure even to eat* 'They had no time even for meals' (We).

6:34 *As he went ashore he saw a great throng, and he had compassion on them* 'Instead of being moved with displeasure because they disturbed him when he desired to be private, as many a man, many a good man, would have been' (H).

The story of the feeding of the multitude was evidently highly prized in the early Church since it is repeated six times in the gospels. (The feeding of the 4000 is presumably a variant of the present story.) In John 6 the story is followed by a discourse of Jesus about the bread of life. Mark leaves his readers to infer its significance, with which indeed they were surely already familiar. It is certainly rich in meaning, and not merely a 'pleasant tale of a picnic in the hills'! For one thing it recalled the way in which God had fed his ancient people with manna in the wilderness, and would give assurance that he could always be relied upon to meet the needs of his people and would never allow them to perish in the desert of this world.

Then again, it was part of the messianic expectation that the coming of God's kingdom would be inaugurated with a mystical banquet – see Isaiah 25:6-8. The so-called First Book of Enoch, which was well-known in the time of Christ, has this passage: 'And the righteous and elect shall be saved in that day . . . and the Lords of Spirits will abide over them, and with that Son of Man shall they eat and lie down and rise up for ever and ever.' Thus the feeding of the multitude may have been regarded as an anticipation of the messianic banquet or as a sacramental promise of the blessed life in God's eternal kingdom. According to John 6:14f. it generated great excitement.

Anyhow, when the story was read at the Christian eucharist it will have been seen to have foreshadowed the Lord's Supper and the holy communion. The Lord himself was always the host and, as the disciples here distributed food, so the deacons distributed the eucharistic gifts in the Christian assemblies. 'Bread and fish appear frequently in frescoes in the catacombs as symbols of the Eucharist' (Br). It is more profitable to reflect on the significance of the story than to ask what actually happened, which is surely irrecoverable.

Some modern teachers have tried to explain the story or to explain it away, but not with very convincing results. (i) The least plausible theory is that the crowd themselves really had provisions which they concealed until they were shamed by the example of the disciples in producing theirs. (ii) Another theory is that a discourse of Jesus about the bread of life was transformed into a miracle story on the basis of the Old Testament precedents, e.g. 2 Kings 4:42f. The O.T. may have influenced the way the story is told, but it is unlikely to have created it. (iii) A more plausible suggestion is that the crowd was satisfied sacramentally, as Christians are in the holy communion, and that the A.V. and R.V. expressions 'and they were filled' is misleading.

6:40 *They sat down in groups, by hundreds and by fifties* This would facilitate counting them, and it is possible that the early Christian communities were arranged thus for the eucharistic feast. The word unimaginatively translated 'groups' literally means 'garden plots' or 'flower beds'. Christopher Wordsworth took advantage of this pleasant fact to comment: 'Our Lord, who then multiplied the five loaves to be food for five thousand, is the same Divine Person who, in a manner less striking, because more gradual and regular, but certainly not less wonderful, ripens all the seeds in all the gardens and orchards, and in all the vineyards and meadows of this world, in successive seasons, ever since man dwelt in Paradise, to minister food to his creatures.'

6:41 *He looked up to heaven, and blessed, and broke the loaves*

The celebrant at mass still looks up like that before consecrating the bread. The customary Jewish blessing was: 'Blessed art thou, o Lord, our God, King of the world, who bringest forth bread from the earth.' – cp. Deuteronomy 8:10. The host or head of the family said the blessing holding the bread, and then broke it and ate a piece himself before distributing it. Have not Christians something to learn from Jews about saying grace at meals?

6:42 *And they all ate* 'With the morsel of bread which he gives his disciples to distribute to the people he consecrates them as partakers in the coming messianic feast, and gives them the guarantee that they, who had shared his table in the time of his obscurity, would also share it in the time of his glory' (A. Schweitzer).

6:43 *And they took up twelve baskets full of broken pieces* Twelve because of the twelve disciples, each of whom has taken one round. What was over symbolizes the inexhaustible abundance of God's grace, like the wine at the wedding at Cana.

45 Immediately he made his disciples get into the boat and go before him to the other side, to Bethsaida, while he dismissed the crowd. 46 And after he had taken leave of them, he went up on the mountain to pray. 47 And when evening came, the boat was out on the sea,

and he was alone on the land. 48 And he saw that they were making headway painfully, for the wind was against them. And about the fourth watch of the night he came to them, walking on the sea. He meant to pass by them, 49 but when they saw him walking on the sea they thought it was a ghost, and cried out; 50 for they all saw him, and were terrified. But immediately he spoke to them and said, 'Take heart, it is I; have no fear.' 51 And he got into the boat with them and the wind ceased. And they were utterly astounded, 52 for they did not understand about the loaves, but their hearts were hardened.

A. E. J. Rawlinson, who supposes Mark to have composed the gospel shortly after the martyrdom of Peter and Paul, vividly imagined the background against which he would have told this story of the crossing of the lake: 'To the Roman church thus bereft of its leaders and confronted by a hostile government, it must indeed have appeared that *the wind was contrary* and progress difficult and slow; faint hearts may even have begun to wonder whether the Lord himself had not abandoned them to their fate . . . They are to learn from this story that they are *not* forsaken, that the Lord watches over them unseen, and that he himself – no phantom but the Living One, Master of winds and waves – will surely come quickly for their salvation.'

6:45 *While he dismissed the crowd* 'Now they had got a good supper, they were in no haste to leave him' (H).

6:48 *About the fourth watch of the night* i.e. about 3 a.m. Mark follows the Roman reckoning which had four night watches. The Jews had only three. *Walking on the sea* The Greek words could mean 'by the sea', and some have supposed that Jesus was walking along the shore and in the misty darkness may have appeared to be walking on the water. But this is not what Mark intended to say. *He meant to pass by them* No satisfactory explana-

tion of these words has been proposed. Sch comments:
'They were meant to see something of his *glory*, like Moses
when God's glory "passed by" him on Mt Sinai (Exodus
33:21-23), or like Elijah on Horeb when the Lord passed
by him in a soft whisper (1 Kings 19:11f.).'

6:51f. *And they were utterly astounded, for they did
not understand* 'Their amazement would have been far
less, had they realized the wonder of the preceding miracle'
(Sw). 'The thought of the evangelist is that the disciples
were not permitted to understand these events until after
the resurrection' (Br).

53 And when they had crossed over, they came to
land at Gennesaret, and moored to the shore. 54 And
when they got out of the boat, immediately the people
recognized him, 55 and ran about the whole neighbourhood and began to bring sick people on their pallets to
any place where they heard he was. 56 And wherever
he came, in villages, cities, or country, they laid the
sick in the market places, and besought him that they
might touch even the fringe of his garment; and as many
as touched it were made well.

This is a summary statement composed by Mark. The
enthusiasm of the crowds offsets the hostility of the Jewish
authorities, of which we are to have further examples in
chapter 7.

6:53 *Gennesaret* Either a fertile plain to the south-west
of Capernaum or else a village situated in it.

6:56 *That they might touch even the fringe of his garment* This was the blue fringe or tassel which every
Israelite man wore on the corner of his robe and by which
every Jew could be distinguished from a Gentile. (See
Numbers 15:37ff.; Deuteronomy 22:12.) It appears that
however much Jesus may have criticized the pharisaic attitude to the Law, he himself observed it.

Some Christians favour wearing on their clothes some

indication or sign that testifies to their faith. Is it desirable that Christians should be distinguishable from non-Christians in some such way?

7:1 Now when the Pharisees gathered together to him, with some of the scribes, who had come from Jerusalem, 2 they saw that some of his disciples ate with hands defiled, that is unwashed. 3 (For the Pharisees, and all the Jews, do not eat unless they wash their hands, observing the tradition of the elders; 4 and when they come from the market place, they do not eat unless they purify themselves; and there are many other traditions which they observe, the washing of cups and pots and vessels of bronze.) 5 And the Pharisees and the scribes asked him, 'Why do your disciples not live according to the tradition of the elders, but eat with hands defiled?' 6 And he said to them, 'Well did Isaiah prophesy of you hypocrites, as it is written,

"This people honours me with their lips,
　　but their heart is far from me;
7　in vain do they worship me,
　　teaching as doctrines the precepts of men."

8 You leave the commandment of God, and hold fast the tradition of men.'

In the first part of this chapter Mark gives some further examples of the teaching of Jesus. Although the question whether Christians were bound to observe the Jewish law had been settled well before this gospel was composed, thanks to the firm stand of St Paul, it still seems to have been a matter of controversy at Rome where the Jewish community is said to have been predominantly pharisaic.

7:2 *With hands defiled, that is, unwashed* i.e. ceremonially unclean.

7:3f. These verses are an editorial explanation for the benefit of Mark's gentile readers. *And all the Jews* is an

exaggeration which may be due to the stance of the Jews
in Rome. The point is that alongside the Law proper (the
Torah) there had grown up an elaborate and detailed code
of practice that was designed to secure rigid obedience to
it. This is described as *the tradition of the elders*. A second-
century A.D. formulation of it has survived in the Jewish
work known as the Mishnah. One cannot be sure that all
the regulations it prescribes go back to the time of Jesus,
but no doubt the hand-washing requirements did so.
Unless they wash their hands This expression is qualified
in the Greek by a word of which both the spelling and
the translation are uncertain, as is shown in the various
English versions, thus: 'oft' (A.V.); 'diligently' (R.V.);
'thoroughly' Wi; 'scrupulously' (New American Bible);
'again and again' (K); 'up to the wrist' (M); 'as far as the
elbow' (J); Goodspeed and Phillips play for safety by
translating: 'in a particular way', and R.S.V. by ignoring
the word altogether. *When they come from the market
place* where they may have rubbed shoulders with Gentiles.
But an alternative translation is possible which should
read: 'they do not eat anything from the market place
unless they sprinkle it'.

7:6f *You hypocrites* the word originally meant a play-
actor and then a pretender or dissembler. Bengel justly remarks that 'we may derive from this passage a definition
of hypocrisy'. The quotation from Isaiah (29:13) depends
on the LXX and will not go back to Jesus, who would not
have used the Greek version.

7:8 *You leave the commandments of God* This looks to
the following verses. Jesus meant that he could cite many
cases in which the Law of God was in effect nullified by
captious interpretation (Lo). He proceeds to give an alleged
instance of this in relation to the fifth commandment.

9 And he said to them, 'You have a fine way of re-
jecting the commandment of God, in order to keep your
tradition! 10 For Moses said, "Honour your father
and your mother"; and, "He who speaks evil of father

or mother, let him surely die"; 11 but you say, "If a man tells his father or his mother, What you would have gained from me is Corban" (that is, given to God) – 12 then you no longer permit him to do anything for his father or mother, 13 thus making void the word of God through your tradition which you hand on. And many such things you do.'

7:11 *Corban* is a Hebrew word, meaning a gift consecrated to God, to be used for religious purposes. The Law laid down the duty of honouring and caring for parents, but according to this passage the Pharisees taught that a vow which declared as dedicated to the Temple whatever might have been given for the support of parents, took precedence of the fifth commandment. (Cp. Deuteronomy 23:21.) Actually the Mishnah shows that at least by the second century A.D. the rabbis agreed with Jesus and allowed that if a vow prevented a man from supporting his parents he should break the vow. As it stands this passage may therefore be unfair to pharisaic teaching, but when Jesus spoke there may have been an allusion to some *cause célèbre* which would have thrown light on what is a somewhat puzzling matter.

14 And he called the people to him again, and said to them, 'Hear me, all of you, and understand: 15 there is nothing outside a man which by going into him can defile him; but the things which come out of a man are what defile him.' 17 And when he had entered the house, and left the people, his disciples asked him about the parable. 18 And he said to them, 'Then are you also without understanding? Do you not see that whatever goes into a man from outside cannot defile him, 19 since it enters, not his heart but his stomach, and so passes on?' (Thus he declared all foods clean.) 20 And he said, 'What comes out of a man is what defiles a man. 21 For from within, out of the heart of man, come evil thoughts, fornication, theft, murder, adultery, 22 coveting,

wickedness, deceit, licentiousness, envy, slander, pride, foolishness. 23 All these evil things come from within, and they defile a man.'

The only kind of cleanliness that matters is moral cleanliness, whereas much of Old Testament Law was based on the importance of ceremonial cleanliness. It is doubtful whether Jesus during his ministry abrogated the ceremonial law in such emphatic terms as Mark represents him as having done, for in that case the long controversy on the subject in the early Church would have been unaccountable. So there may be some exaggeration here; some special case may have been in view. Anyhow, what is said here was the eventual outcome of the Lord's teaching.

7:14 *He called the people* 'In Mark the people are never far away, and can be addressed at will' (Gr).

7:17 *When he had entered the house* This is a favourite way Mark has of adding to teaching which he considered required further explanation. *Parable* here is used in the sense of an enigmatic saying.

7:19 *And so passes on* i.e. into the privy or latrine, which is what the Greek says. 'The natural process is spoken of with unselfconscious naturalness' (Cr). *Thus he declared all foods clean* i.e. he did away with the judaic distinction of meats. This is Mark's comment. (Cp. Acts 10, Peter's vision.)

7:20f. Lists of this sort were a common feature of ethical teaching in the Hellenistic world. *Envy* i.e. jealousy. *Foolishness* in the Bible is a moral rather than an intellectual failing.

24 And from there he arose and went away to the region of Tyre and Sidon. And he entered a house, and would not have any one know it; yet he could not be hid. 25 But immediately a woman, whose little daughter was possessed by an unclean spirit, heard of him, and came and fell down at his feet. 26 Now the woman was a

Greek, a Syrophoenician by birth. And she begged him to cast the demon out of her daughter. 27 And he said to her, 'Let the children first be fed, for it is not right to take the children's bread and throw it to the dogs.' 28 But she answered him, 'Yes, Lord; yet even the dogs under the table eat the children's crumbs.' 29 And he said to her, 'For this saying you may go your way; the demon has left your daughter.' 30 And she went home, and found the child lying in bed, and the demon gone.

7:24 *He . . . went away to the region of Tyre and Sidon* i.e. the territory to the north of Galilee. *And Sidon* should be omitted. The purpose of the journey is not stated. Some have thought it was the start of a mission to Gentiles, but there is insufficient evidence for this supposition. Naturally in the early Church there was a welcome for any stories that showed Jesus extending his mission to Gentiles and not confining it to Israel. This story seems to have been one of the few at Mark's disposal that pointed in that direction, though it does so in an ambiguous manner. In reality, Jesus appears to have addressed his ministry to Jews; it was God's plan that its scope should become universal subsequently. *He entered a house, and would not have any one know it* i.e. he was seeking privacy, but seeking it in vain.

7:26 *The woman was a Greek, a Syrophoenician by birth* i.e. a Gentile and Greek-speaking, and a Syrian from the Phoenician coast.

7:27 *Let the children first be fed* i.e. the children of Israel. *And throw it to the dogs.* The Jews commonly spoke opprobiously of the Gentiles as dogs. It is true that Mark uses a diminutive which means 'little dogs', but then he was fond of diminutives and there is no corresponding word in Aramaic. Rawlinson writes: 'The words are probably spoken by our Lord half whimsically, and with a smile . . . He wanted to see what the woman would say if he affected to adopt the conventional Jewish point of view.' T. R. Glover conjectured that 'the allusion to dogs has been thrown back into Jesus's words from the woman's reply, and that she was the first to mention them'; but this seems like special pleading.

7:28 *But she answered* Her persistence was evidence of her faith in Jesus. *Yet even the dogs under the table* 'Arguing great subtlety on the part of the woman,' says Bengel, 'she alleges as an argument the nearness of her country to Israel; as of the dogs to their master's table.' *Eat the children's crumbs* These may have been waste pieces of bread on which the guests wiped their hands after eating and then threw to the dogs.

For Mark and his readers this story symbolized or anticipated the spread of the Gospel among the Gentiles, and the fact that the cure was effected at a distance could be taken to mean that the Gentiles would be saved by the word without the bodily presence of Christ.

31 Then he returned from the region of Tyre, and went through Sidon to the Sea of Galilee, through the region of the Decapolis. 32 And they brought to him a man who was deaf and had an impediment in his speech; and they besought him to lay his hands upon him. 33 And taking him aside from the multitude privately, he put his fingers into his ears, and he spat and touched his tongue; 34 and looking up to heaven he sighed and said to him, '*Ephphatha*', that is, 'Be opened.' 35 And his ears were opened, his tongue was released, and he spoke plainly. 36 And he charged them to tell no one; but the more he charged them, the more zealously they proclaimed it. 37 And they were astonished beyond measure, saying, 'He has done all things well; he even makes the deaf hear and the dumb speak.'

7:31 The geographical details in this verse, for which Mark was responsible, are very improbable. They have been compared to a journey from London to Cornwall via Manchester! Cranfield's remark that 'it is possible that this verse reflects a certain vagueness on Mark's part about the geography of northern Palestine' is a masterly understatement. Mark's readers in Rome will not have been better informed.

7:32 *A man who was deaf and had an impediment in his speech* 'a deaf man that stammered' (We).

7:33f. The gesture and healing methods used by Jesus were well-known in the ancient world, especially in the sphere of magic.

7:35 *He spoke plainly* The man had not been completely dumb, though this is often described as 'the healing of a deaf mute'.

7:37 These were the kind of miracles that were expected of the Messiah, see Isaiah 35:5f.

8:1 In those days, when again great crowds had gathered, and they had nothing to eat, he called his disciples to him, and said to them, 2 'I have compassion on the crowd, because they have been with me now three days, and have nothing to eat; 3 and if I send them away hungry to their homes, they will faint on the way; and some of them have come a long way.' 4 And his disciples answered him, 'How can one feed these men with bread here in the desert?' 5 And he asked them, 'How many loaves have you?' They said, 'Seven.' 6 And he commanded the crowd to sit down on the ground; and he took the seven loaves, and having given thanks he broke them and gave them to his disciples to set before the people; and they set them before the crowd. 7 And they had a few small fish; and having blessed them, he commanded that these also should be set before them. 8 And they ate, and were satisfied; and they took up the broken pieces left over, seven baskets full. 9 And there were about four thousand people. 10 And he sent them away; and immediately he got into the boat with his disciples, and went to the district of Dalmanutha.

This is almost certainly a variant of the previous story of the feeding of the multitude (6:35-44). Apart from any other consideration, if the disciples had already experienced the previous miracle, it is unbelievable that they should react as they do here in v. 4. The question therefore is why does Mark, whose space was limited, record two versions of the same story? The best answer is that he intended the feeding of the five thousand to symbolize the bringing of the Gospel and its blessing to the Jews, and the feeding of the four thousand to the Gentiles. Not only does this second feeding take place on gentile territory, but there may be symbolism in the numbers. The five thousand receive the five loaves, which can represent the five books of the Jewish Law (the Pentateuch); the four thousand receive seven loaves with which may be compared the seventy nations of the gentile world (see Genesis 10) and the mission of the seventy disciples in Luke 10:1, which represents the mission to the gentile world in contrast to his account of the previous mission of the twelve (Luke 9:1). Further symbolism of this kind has been detected in the two narratives.

8:6f. *Having given thanks . . . and having blessed them* Different Greek words, the former being *eucharistesas* from which 'eucharist' is derived. 'They do right in taking food, who pray over the several courses' (Be).

8:10 *The district of Dalmanutha* No such place is known; see note on 7:31.

8:11 The Pharisees came and began to argue with him, seeking from him a sign from heaven, to test him. 12 And he sighed deeply in his spirit, and said, 'Why does this generation seek a sign? Truly, I say to you, no sign shall be given to this generation.' 13 And he left them, and getting into the boat again he departed to the other side.

8:11 *The Pharisees came* They appear from nowhere. *Seeking from him a sign from heaven* – presumably a flash of lightning, or a clap of thunder, or a voice from heaven. Prophets and teachers were asked to produce signs of this kind to substantiate their authority. *To test him.* If he could not produce a sign, that would be an avowal of his lack of power.

8:12 *No sign shall be given* It is not easy to reconcile this with the exorcisms and healings that Jesus had performed as evidence that the kingdom of God has drawn near. It may however be said that 'a sign such as they desire will not be given – though signs of God's choosing are indeed being given' (Cr). It is not for men to determine when and in what form signs shall be given.

14 Now they had forgotten to bring bread; and they had only one loaf with them in the boat. 15 And he cautioned them, saying, 'Take heed, beware of the leaven of the Pharisees and the leaven of Herod.' 16 And they discussed it with one another, saying, 'We have no bread.' 17 And being aware of it, Jesus said to them, 'Why do you discuss the fact that you have no bread? Do you not yet perceive or understand? Are your hearts hardened? 18 Having eyes do you not see, and having ears do you not hear? And do you not remember? 19 When I broke the five loaves for the five thousand, how many baskets full of broken pieces did you take up?' They said to him, 'Twelve.' 20 'And the seven for the four thousand, how many baskets full of broken pieces did you take up?' And they said to him, 'Seven.' 21 And he said to them, 'Do you not yet understand?'

8:15 This verse should be in brackets. Luke (12:1) has it in a different context; it was apparently an isolated saying that was inserted here because of the connection between leaven and bread. The rabbis used leaven as a metaphor for the evil tendencies in man (cp. 1 Corinthians 5:6ff.; Galatians 5:9). *Of the Pharisees and . . . of Herod* 'Two opposite extremes of religious sects' (Be) – of religiosity, on the one hand, and of worldliness, on the other (?).

8:16 *We have no bread* They ought to have realized, after the two miracles which they are said to have experienced, that Jesus could supply their needs from one loaf – and indeed that he could meet all human needs.

8:17 *Do you not yet perceive or understand?* The gospels, not least Mark's, are very frank about the disciples' obtuseness and lack of understanding. No doubt there were many such hearers in the churches of the evangelists' time, and preachers may have found a passage like this useful for upbraiding them and stirring them to deeper perception.

22 And they came to Bethsaida. And some people brought to him a blind man, and begged him to touch him. 23 And he took the blind man by the hand, and led him out of the village; and when he had spit on his eyes and laid his hands upon him, he asked him, 'Do you see anything?' 24 And he looked up and said, 'I see men; but they look like trees, walking.' 25 Then again he laid his hands upon his eyes; and he looked intently and was restored, and saw everything clearly. 26 And he sent him away to his home, saying, 'Do not even enter the village.'

This story of the healing of a blind man is so similar to that of 7:31-37 that some have thought that they are variants of the same. This one is omitted by Matthew and Luke, perhaps for that reason, or because the cure here is only gradual.

8:23 *Led him out of the village* In fact Bethsaida was a considerable town, but some areas of towns and cities have been known as 'villages'.

8:24 *I see men; but they look like trees, walking* Other translations of this vivid saying are: 'I can see people; they look like trees to me, but they are walking about' (J); 'I can make out people, for I see them as large as trees, moving' (M). We can compare *Macbeth* (v. 5. 34ff.):

As I did stand my watch upon the hill,
I looked towards Birnam, and anon methought
The wood began to move.

8:26 *Do not even enter the village* A better reading is:
'Do not tell anyone in the village.'

It may be significant that this story of the restoration
of a man's sight precedes what appears to be a new section
of the gospel (8:27-10:52) in which the truth about Jesus
is going to be gradually made clear to the disciples.

27 And Jesus went on with his disciples, to the villages
of Caesarea Philippi; and on the way he asked his disciples, 'Who do men say that I am?' 28 And they told
him, 'John the Baptist; and others say Elijah; and others
one of the prophets.' 29 And he asked them, 'But who
do you say that I am?' Peter answered him, 'You are
the Christ.' 30 And he charged them to tell no one about
him.

From this point in the gospel Jesus is represented as no
longer addressing the public but as concentrating on the
training and enlightenment of the disciples. Moreover, the
emphasis now is increasingly on the inevitability of suffering and what has been described as 'the shadow of the
cross'. Until now the belief that Jesus was the Messiah,
which Mark certainly held, has been treated as a mysterious
secret, penetrated only by the demons who were thought
to have supernatural knowledge, and otherwise only
vaguely hinted at. 'The theme of suffering, already hinted
at once or twice, is now fully sounded – not in the whisper-
ing woodwinds but in the harsh, deep-throated brass'
(Gr). Now for the first time Jesus is to be identified as
the Messiah, albeit in a qualified or ambiguous manner.

8:27 The locality is vaguely indicated. This Caesarea,
situated on the slopes of Mount Hermon and at the source
of the River Jordan, was called 'Philippi', i.e. of Philip, to
distinguish it from the Caesarea on the Mediterranean

coast. It had been rebuilt by Herod Philip and so named after him. *The villages of Caesarea Philippi* may mean the hamlets surrounding the town.

8:29 *But who do you say that I am?* The *you* is emphatic. 'Some people say one thing, and others something else, but who do *you* say that I am?' *You*, who form the nucleus of the new Israel; *you*, to whom it has been given to know the mysteries of the kingdom of God; *you*, whom I have called and chosen, who do *you* say that I am? *Peter answered him, 'You are the Christ'*, i.e. the Messiah, see note on 1:1. Jesus neither accepts nor declines the designation, because at this stage it could easily be misunderstood.

8.30 *He charged them to tell no one about him* (or *about it*) There were, as we have seen, various messianic expectations of a political messiah who would establish his kingdom by force, or of an apocalyptic figure who would descend on the clouds of heaven. Jesus could not openly or unreservedly accept the designation until the meaning of his messiahship had been explained and understood. His vocation as Messiah was to suffer and give up his life for his people. 'There may, accordingly, be a double implication in this verse: (a) Jesus really *is* the Messiah, but in another sense than everyone supposed at the time; (b) the public announcement of his messiahship, without this reinterpretation, would only lead to misunderstanding' (Gr). So from now onwards in Mark's gospel, the disciples are being educated into an understanding of the necessity of suffering and of the cross as a way of life.

31 And he began to teach them that the Son of man must suffer many things, and be rejected by the elders and the chief priests and the scribes, and be killed, and after three days rise again. 32 And he said this plainly. And Peter took him, and began to rebuke him. 33 But turning and seeing his disciples, he rebuked Peter, and said, 'Get behind me, Satan! For you are not on the

side of God, but of men.' 34 And he called to him the
multitude with his disciples, and said to them, 'If any
man would come after me, let him deny himself and take
up his cross and follow me. 35 For whoever would save
his life will lose it,; and whoever loses his life for my
sake and the gospel's will save it. 36 For what does it
profit a man, to gain the whole world and forfeit his
life? 37 For what can a man give in return for his life?
38 For whoever is ashamed of me and of my words in
this adulterous and sinful generation, of him will the Son
of man also be ashamed, when he comes in the glory
of his Father with the holy angels.'

8:31 *The Son of man must suffer many things* (On *the
Son of man* see the note on 2:10.) This is the first of three
solemn predictions of the passion that is approaching
(see also 9:30; 10:32). They have been strikingly compared
to the tolling of a minute bell as the party makes its way
from the slopes of Hermon to Jerusalem in the south.
After three days could be a conventional expression for
'after a short period'. Or the terms of the prediction may
have been influenced by what actually happened in the
event. It is one thing to say that Jesus was confident that
God would vindicate him, another to suppose that he fore-
saw precisely how this would come about.

8:32 *He said this plainly* i.e. 'frankly', rather than
'openly' as A.V. and R.V. have it. *Peter . . . began to rebuke him* 'You mustn't talk like that, Master.'

8:33 *Get behind me, Satan!* 'Get behind me, Adversary'
(We). Jesus regards Peter's attitude as a temptation, an
attempt to draw him away from the path of obedience
to his Father's will. Perhaps it should be translated: 'Get
out of my sight, Satan!' It is the same temptation as was
put to Jesus in the wilderness (see 1:13).

8:34ff. Not only is the Messiah called to suffering but
so too are those who would follow him. The lesson was
specially relevant to the church in Rome, exposed as it
was to persecution. *Take up his cross* 'The Romans re-

quired a condemned criminal to carry part of his own cross to the place of execution; hence the metaphor' (N). It meant 'to venture on a life which is as difficult as the last walk of a man condemned to death' (Sch). The disciple must be ready to face martyrdom. These verses are to be seen as a warning, not as an irrevocable sentence.

8:38 *Whoever is ashamed of me* i.e. whoever does not understand the mystery of the passion, but regards the cross as a scandal or as an obstacle to faith. From the earliest days Christians have been ridiculed for their faith, and ridicule is very hard to bear. *In this adulterous . . . generation* i.e. idolatrous, as often in the Old Testament. This verse at first sight distinguishes between Jesus and the Son of man, but that cannot be what Mark intended. Jesus is speaking here to the multitude (see v. 34), and not only to the disciples, so he is represented as being careful to keep his messiahship secret or veiled. As Bengel points out: 'concerning the present time, he speaks in the first person; concerning the future, in the third'.

9:1 And he said to them, 'Truly, I say to you, there are some standing here who will not taste death before they see that the kingdom of God has come with power.'

This verse was originally independent, and Mark probably inserted it here because he saw in the Transfiguration, which he is about to relate, a partial fulfilment of it. But *the kingdom of God has come with power* properly meant what is known as the *parousia* or the final coming of the kingdom in glory. There are good reasons for thinking that Jesus did say that this consummation was to take place in the proximate future, as the primitive Christians certainly expected that it would. 'There is every reason to think that Jesus proclaimed that the Divine Event was near. But it is very doubtful if he formulated any such exact chronology of its arrival as the passage here presents' (Br). In the case of Christ himself this prophetic foreshortening of the future will have been an instance of the limitation of his human knowledge that was involved in his becoming man, sometimes known as his self-emptying or *kenosis* (see Philippians 2:7; see also note on 13:30 below).

2 And after six days Jesus took with him Peter and James and John, and led them up a high mountain apart by themselves; and he was transfigured before them, 3 and his garments became glistening, intensely white, as no fuller on earth could bleach them. 4 And there appeared to them Elijah with Moses; and they were talking to Jesus. 5 And Peter said to Jesus, 'Master, it is well that we are here; let us make three booths, one for you and one for Moses and one for Elijah.' 6 For he did not know what to say, for they were exceedingly afraid. 7 And a cloud overshadowed them, and a voice came out of the cloud, 'This is my beloved Son; listen to him.' 8 And suddenly looking around they no longer saw any one with them but Jesus only.

This story of the Transfiguration has been regarded by some as an account of an appearance of Jesus after the resurrection, which Mark has transposed to this place. Whatever the origin of the story, and from whatever experience, factual or visionary, it may derive, Mark evidently inserts it here because he looked upon it as a divine attestation or confirmation of the truth which Peter had blurted out. His words, 'Thou art the Christ', are now ratified from the cloud, i.e. by the voice of God himself: *'This is my beloved Son; listen to him.'*

9:2 *And after six days* Mark rarely gives notes of time. His intention here seems to be to link the Transfiguration with Peter's confession – but see also Exodus 24:15f., which may have influenced this story. In the New Testament Jesus is widely regarded as the new Moses (cp. Deuteronomy 18:18). *A high mountain* Mountains had long been looked upon as the appropriate setting for divine revelations or theophanies (see note on 3:13). *He was trans-*

figured The word 'means a change of form, an effulgence from within, not a mere "flood of glory" from without . . . a manifestation of the Son of God in his true nature as he will be seen on the last day' (Gr). 'The transfiguration points forward to, and is as it were a foretaste of, the Resurrection, which in turn points forward to, and is a foretaste of, the Parousia' (Cr).

9:3 *His garments became glistening* For the brightness of clothing in connection with glory, see Daniel 7:9; Revelation 3:5; 7:9. In 1 Enoch it is said that the elect will be clothed in garments of glory from the lord of spirits, and their glory shall never fade away. *As no fuller on earth could bleach them* 'With a whiteness with which no earthly laundering could whiten them' (Ba). This is meant to stress the divine or heavenly origin of what was happening.

9:4 *There appeared to them Elijah with Moses* Elijah is mentioned first as the attendant or companion of Moses. There was an expectation that both would reappear in the last days. Their appearance means that both the Law and the prophets testify to Jesus as the Christ (cp. Luke 24:44). 'Moses and Elias lived at a great distance of time from one another; but that breaks no squares in heaven, where all are one in Christ' (H).

9:5 *It is well that we are here*, otherwise there would be no one to do honour to these mysterious visitants. *Let us make three booths* either shelters such as were used at the feast of tabernacles or tents. 'The words may simply express a desire on Peter's part to prolong the blessedness of the experience when in fact it was God's will for Christ and his disciples that they should return into the world and enter upon the path of suffering' (N). Or does Peter suppose that the messianic age has arrived when God will dwell with his people (see Ezekiel 37:27; Zechariah 2:10f.)?

9:6 *He did not know what to say* He hardly knew what to say because he was so dazed and awed by the vision.

9:7 *And a cloud overshadowed them* A cloud was a well-known symbol of the divine presence (see e.g. Exodus 16:10; Numbers 11:25). The meaning may be that the cloud concealed Jesus, Moses and Elijah from the three disciples. *A voice came out of the cloud* A heavenly echo of Peter's confession, and a reiteration of the voice at the baptism (1:11).

9:8 *They no longer saw any one . . . but Jesus only* Law and prophecy now pass away and he alone remains. 'The representatives of the old dispensation . . . yield place to him who as the author of the new dispensation now fulfils them both' (Li).

9 And as they were coming down the mountain, he charged them to tell no one what they had seen, until the Son of man should have risen from the dead. 10 So they kept the matter to themselves, questioning what the rising from the dead meant. 11 And they asked him, 'Why do the scribes say that first Elijah must come?' 12 And he said to them, 'Elijah does come first to restore all things; and how is it written of the Son of man, that he should suffer many things, and be treated with contempt? 13 But I tell you that Elijah has come, and they did to him whatever they pleased, as it is written of him.'

9:10 *Questioning what the rising from the dead meant* It will not have been the idea of resurrection that puzzled them, for the Jews for two centuries had been familiar with that, but the death and resurrection of the Son of man. It seems that v. 12b (*How is it written of the Son of man . . .?*) has got out of place and should follow v. 10

9:11 *Why do the scribes say that first Elijah must come?* Mark may have considered that the question was prompted either by 9:1 or by Elijah's appearance in the Transfiguration scene – see Malachi 4:5f., from which apparently the surprising idea that Elijah would 'restore all things' is derived; see also Mark 1:1f, and note there. John 1:21

says definitely that John was not Elijah. Questions about his coming were still exercising people's minds in the second century A.D. Justin Martyr, who composed a dialogue between a Christian and a Jew (Trypho, by name), has a whole chapter on the subject.

9:13 *As it is written of him* Is the reference here to 1 Kings 19:2, 10 or perhaps to some lost apocryphal writing? M. Henry avoided the difficulty by saying that the words applied to the coming of Elijah, and that the clause *and they did to him whatever they pleased* is a parenthesis and should be in brackets.

14 And when they came to the disciples, they saw a great crowd about them, and scribes arguing with them. 15 And immediately all the crowd, when they saw him, were greatly amazed, and ran up to him and greeted him. 16 And he asked them, 'What are you discussing with them?' 17 And one of the crowd answered him, 'Teacher, I brought my son to you, for he has a dumb spirit; 18 and wherever it seizes him, it dashes him down; and he foams and grinds his teeth and becomes rigid; and I asked your disciples to cast it out, and they were not able.' 19 And he answered them, 'O faithless generation, how long am I to be with you? How long am I to bear with you? Bring him to me.' 20 And they brought the boy to him; and when the spirit saw him, immediately it convulsed the boy, and he fell on the ground and rolled about, foaming at the mouth. 21 And Jesus asked his father, 'How long has he had this?' And he said, 'From childhood. 22 And it has often cast him into the fire and into the water, to destroy him; but if you can do anything, have pity on us and help us.' 23 And Jesus said to him, 'If you can! All things are possible to him who believes.' 24 Immediately the father of the child cried out and said, 'I believe; help my unbelief!' 25 And when Jesus saw that a crowd came running together, he rebuked the unclean spirit, saying to it, 'You dumb and deaf spirit, I command you, come out of him, and never

enter him again.' 26 And after crying out and convulsing him terribly, it came out, and the boy was like a
corpse; so that most of them said, 'He is dead.' 27 But
Jesus took him by the hand and lifted him up, and he
arose. 28 And when he had entered the house, his
disciples asked him privately, 'Why could we not cast
it out?' 29 And he said to them, 'This kind cannot be
driven out by anything but prayer.'

9:14 *When they came* i.e. Jesus, Peter, James and
John.

9:15 *All the crowd, when they saw him, were greatly
amazed* Why? 'Probably there might remain something unusual in his countenance: as Moses's face shone when he
came down from the mount, Exodus 34:30, so perhaps
did Christ's face in some measure; at least, instead of seem-
ing fatigued, there appeared a wonderful briskness and
sprightliness in his looks, which amazed them' (H). Or
was their astonishment 'due to Jesus's unexpected and opportune arrival' (Cr), 'the impressive arrival of the wonder-
worker in the nick of time' (Br)?

9:18 The symptoms described point to epilepsy. *Becomes rigid* may mean 'becomes exhausted'.

9:19 *O faithless generation* 'A whole world of dis-
belief in the way of the boy's restoration' (Gr). This
apostrophe echoes the laments of Old Testament prophets
and the experience of Moses when he descended from
Mount Sinai (Exodus 32).

9:23 *If you can!* Jesus repeats the father's words in order
to question them.

9:24 *I believe; help my unbelief!* 'The memorable,
haunting cry of the father . . . the words have brought
consolation, as no doubt St Mark intended them to do, to
countless Christians conscious of the inadequacy of their
own faith' (N). 'He declares that he *believes*, and yet ac-
knowledges himself to have *unbelief*. These two statements appear to contradict each other, but there is none
of us that does not experience both of them in himself'
(C).

9:25 *You dumb and deaf spirit* These infirmities may have been added to the marks of epilepsy in order to heighten the effect of the miracle. The boy represents mankind delivered by Christ from its spiritual infirmities and enabled to praise God and to hear his word. *And never enter him again* The boy's trouble was not continuous illness but periodic fits.

9:28 *When he had entered the house, his disciples asked him privately* This is Mark's way of showing that there is here a special lesson for the Church, namely the importance of prayer, although there was no mention of prayer on Jesus's part in v. 27.

9:29 *This kind cannot be driven out by anything but prayer* This no doubt reflects the experience of the early Church. It is not the utterance of a single prayer but a life of prayer that is meant. The additional words *and fasting* are not in the most reliable manuscripts and were probably added by an early script editor.

This story of the cure of the epileptic may have been placed here by Mark as a fitting sequel to the Transfiguration, since it showed the Christ, who had just been glorified on the mountain, at once at work again in the plain below. It was a sign to all readers of the gospel that after moments of vision or ecstasy they must be ready to return promptly to the humdrum tasks of life in this world.

30 They went on from there and passed through Galilee. And he would not have any one know it; 31 for he was teaching his disciples, saying to them, 'The Son of man will be delivered into the hands of men, and they will kill him; and when he is killed, after three days he will rise.' 32 But they did not understand the saying, and they were afraid to ask him.

This is the second prediction of the Passion; see note on 8:31.

9:30f. He wanted to be incognito because he was now

fully occupied in training the disciples.

9:32 *They did not understand the saying*, although it could hardly have been plainer. According to Mark they understood Jesus's predictions no more than they understood his parables. This helped to explain why, when the events occurred, the disciples were taken by surprise. *And they were afraid to ask him* perhaps because they remembered how Peter was censured in 8:33. Numerous Christians today seem afraid to ask questions concerning their faith. Why? 'Many remain ignorant, because they are ashamed to enquire' (H).

33 And they came to Capernaum; and when he was in the house he asked them, 'What were you discussing on the way?' 34 But they were silent; for on the way they had discussed with one another who was the greatest. 35 And he sat down and called the twelve; and he said to them, 'If any one would be first, he must be last of all and servant of all.' 36 And he took a child, and put him in the midst of them; and taking him in his arms, he said to them, 37 'Whoever receives one such child in my name receives me; and whoever receives me, receives not me but him who sent me.'

This paragraph, and indeed the remainder of the chapter, deal with various aspects of discipleship.

9:33 *They came to Capernaum*, which is here mentioned for the last time. *In the house* – presumably Peter's house.

9:35 *He sat down* – the posture of a teacher or judge. *If any one would be first* Several sayings like this are attributed to Jesus in the gospels. They will have been of use in the early Church, as they have been ever since, to check personal ambition. But is ambition always to be deprecated?

9:36 *He took a child* The point here lies not in the child's attitude but in the attitude of others towards the child.

9:37 *Whoever receives one such child* 'Shows kindness to', or possibly there is a reference to baptism when the name of Jesus will have been invoked. Otherwise *in my name* could mean 'as a Christian' or 'for my sake'. Anyhow, the saying was, and is, an incentive to hospitality and to the care of orphans.

38 John said to him, 'Teacher, we saw a man casting out demons in your name, and we forbade him, because he was not following us.' 39 But Jesus said, 'Do not forbid him; for no one who does a mighty work in my name will be able soon after to speak evil of me. 40 For he that is not against us is for us. 41 For truly, I say to you, whoever gives you a cup of water to drink because you bear the name of Christ, will by no means lose his reward.'

9:38 *We saw a man casting out demons in your name* 'We saw a man making use of your name to expel demons' (We). This incident may be linked to what precedes because of the reference to 'the name'. Both in the Old Testament and in the gospels sayings were sometimes strung together because of such a verbal connection. In the early Church the question arose of what should be the Christian attitude to non-Christian exorcists who made use of the name of Jesus.

9:39f. 'Jesus's followers were to welcome honest co-operation, even in unexpected places and by irregular means' (Gr). 'Let us give heed to these words, who tie down spiritual gifts to a canonical succession' (Be). 'There are kind people who help others out of common humanity, even though they are not professed Christians; they will experience God's mercy at the judgement' (Sch). 'In religion our exclusions are nearly always wrong, and our inclusions, however inconsistent, nearly always right' (Evelyn Underhill).

9:41 Another saying about 'the name'. 'Christ' was not used as a proper name during the ministry, so this must be a saying that took shape in the early Church. 'Note, they who belong to Christ, may sometimes be reduced to such straits as to be glad of a cup of cold water' (H).

42 'Whoever causes one of these little ones who believe in me to sin, it would be better for him if a great millstone were hung round his neck and he were thrown into the sea. 43 And if your hand causes you to sin, cut it off; it is better for you to enter life maimed than with two hands to go to hell, to the unquenchable fire. 45 And if your foot causes you to sin, cut it off; it is better for you to enter life lame than with two feet to be thrown into hell. 47 And if your eye causes you to sin, pluck it out; it is better for you to enter the kingdom of God with one eye than with two eyes to be thrown into hell, 48 where their worm does not die, and the fire is not quenched. 49 For every one will be salted with fire. 50 Salt is good; but if the salt has lost its saltness, how will you season it? Have salt in yourselves, and be at peace with one another.'

9:42 *Whoever causes one of these little ones who believe in me to sin* or rather 'to stumble', i.e. to cause to fall away from God. Mark is thinking here of simple Christian believers and of those who scorned or scoffed at them, though the saying may originally have had to do with children. The *millstone* in question was a huge one turned by an ass, such as was in common use in the time of Jesus.

9:43-48 *Causes you to sin* It is the same Greek word as in v. 42, 'causes you to stumble', which provides a verbal link between these verses. What they are saying is: 'You must be ready to make the costliest possible sacrifice.' *To be thrown into hell* In view of the ambiguity of the English word 'hell' it is better not to translate the word *Gehenna* but to retain it as Moffatt does. Gehenna was a valley outside Jerusalem, named after the son of Hinnom, where human sacrifices had been offered to Moloch (see Jeremiah

7:31, 32:35). It had been desecrated by King Josiah (see 2 Kings 23:10), and became a dump for the garbage of the city. Hence *where their worm does not die, and the fire is not quenched* (cp. Isaiah 66:24). Phillips boldly translates 'be thrown on to the rubbish heap'. It was not a place of torment, but a place for the disposal of debris.

9:49 *Every one will be salted with fire* 'Fire' is the verbal link here. We do not know the original context of this saying. Salt is both purifying and preservative. The meaning may be that every disciple must be prepared to face the fire of persecution. This part of Mark's gospel resounds with echoes of martyrdom. The words added in A.V., 'and every sacrifice shall be salted with salt', are missing in the best manuscripts. See Leviticus 2:13.

9:50 This verse is not easy to interpret. Salt cannot really lose its saltness, but in Palestine it is said often to have been mixed with other ingredients such as sand. So it can lose its true character while retaining the appearance of salt. Salt may here stand for some astringent qualities that the disciples should possess: cp. Colossians 4:6. *Have salt in yourselves, and be at peace with one another* 'A declaration that the way to peace is a life seasoned with the astringent qualities of salt, perhaps, as we should say, with common sense, appears to be the meaning of the passage' (T).

10:1 And he left there and went to the region of Judea and beyond the Jordan, and crowds gathered to him again; and again, as his custom was, he taught them.

He is now on his way up to Jerusalem and resumes his public ministry. It is implied that he went up to Jerusalem not by Samaria but by Perea (now Transjordan). But the text is uncertain and, as usual, Mark was not well informed about the topography.

2 And Pharisees came up and in order to test him asked, 'Is it lawful for a man to divorce his wife?' 3 He

answered them, 'What did Moses command you?' 4
They said, 'Moses allowed a man to write a certificate of
divorce, and to put her away.' 5 But Jesus said to them,
'For your hardness of heart he wrote you this commandment. 6 But from the beginning of creation, "God
made them male and female." 7 "For this reason a man
shall leave his father and mother and be joined to his
wife, 8 and the two shall become one flesh." So they
are no longer two but one flesh. 9 What therefore
God has joined together, let no man put asunder.' 10
And in the house the disciples asked him again about
this matter. 11 And he said to them, 'Whoever divorces
his wife and marries another, commits adultery against
her; 12 and if she divorces her husband and marries
another, she commits adultery.'

10:2 *In order to test him* or 'to tempt him'. The word
is the same as that used in the Lord's Prayer for 'temptation' or 'time of trial'. Here it can mean either that they
wanted to trip him up by getting him to make a damaging
admission or that they genuinely wanted to ascertain his
opinion about a disputed matter.

10:4 *Moses allowed a man to write a certificate of
divorce* See Deuteronomy 24:1. A later form of such a
certificate read as follows: 'On . . . (date), I . . . (name),
son of . . . and of . . ., of my own free will and purpose
without any coercion whatever, do divorce, set free, and
repudiate you . . . (name), so that you are now free and in
full possession of your own person, with the right to go and
be married to whomever you choose.' Jewish law allowed
a husband to divorce his wife, but not a wife to divorce her
husband. In the time of Jesus there was a controversy
about the grounds for divorce. The school of Shammai
allowed divorce only for adultery, whereas the school of
Hillel was more lenient and allowed divorce for trivial
offences such as burning the bread. Matthew (19:3) as-
sumes that Jesus was being asked to pronounce between
these two schools, but in Mark the question is whether he

approves of divorce at all.

10:5 *For your hardness of heart* means insensibility to the call of God or stubborn rebelliousness against God.

10:6 *But from the beginning of creation* See Genesis 1:27; 2:24. The words can mean 'at the beginning of Genesis'. Anyhow, assuming that both were the work of Moses, Jesus is contrasting Genesis with Deuteronomy and, as it were, appealing to Moses against Moses. He is saying that in the original divine intention marriage was monogamous and indissoluble, and the later concession of divorce was a departure from it. Whether in these verses Jesus should be understood to have been affirming what is the ideal or norm for marriage, *or* to have been promulgating an unbreakable law has always been a vexed question. Already in the New Testament it was recognized that divorce was permissible for Christians in certain circumstances (see Matthew 19:9; 1 Corinthians 7:15), and all churches have in one way or another allowed for exceptions. Has this been culpable or reasonable?

10:10ff. In contrast to Jewish law, Roman law allowed a wife to divorce her husband, and Mark presumably added these verses for the benefit of his Roman readers. He explains that the Lord's teaching forbade either party to divorce the other.

13 And they were bringing children to him, that he might touch them! and the disciples rebuked them. 14 But when Jesus saw it he was indignant, and said to them, 'Let the children come to me, do not hinder them; for to such belongs the kingdom of God. 15 Truly I say to you, whoever does not receive the kingdom of God like a child shall not enter it.' 16 And he took them in his arms and blessed them, laying his hands upon them.

10:13 *And they were bringing children to him* It is widely supposed that this meant mothers bringing their babes. But that is because Luke (18:15), using a different Greek word, says that it was infants that were brought to Jesus. The word Mark uses can mean children of up to twelve years of age, and he probably means that it was boys of about that age and that they were brought by their fathers rather than by their mothers. It has been justly said that it is a safe rule not to introduce women into a Bible scene unless they are specified. This incident is represented as having taken place on the way to Jerusalem. Infants or little children would hardly be taken on the passover pilgrimage. *That he might touch them* i.e. bless them. *And the disciples rebuked them* Why? Because he was tired? Because they thought that he ought not to be bothered with children, 'as one might wish to safeguard a famous man from the embarrassing solicitations of autograph hunters of today' (R)? Or because the disciples did not want the Master's blessing to be given indiscriminately without some preliminary sifting or enquiry (cp. what is called 'indiscriminate baptism' today)?

10:14 *When Jesus saw it he was indignant* 'Was angry' (M) is a better translation. It is a strong word which Matthew and Luke omit. *For to such belongs the kingdom of God* The point is not that children are innocent, humble or obedient, but that they are receptive and content to depend on the care and bounty of others. The kingdom of God is a gift to be received, not an achievement on man's part.

10:16 *He took them in his arms* i.e. he put his arms round the boys. 'See how he outdid the desires of these parents; they begged he would touch them. He did more' (H).

17 And as he was setting out on his journey, a man ran up and knelt before him, and asked him, 'Good teacher, what must I do to inherit eternal life?' 18 And Jesus said to him, 'Why do you call me good? No one is good but God alone. 19 You know the commandments: "Do not kill, Do not commit adultery, Do not steal, Do not bear false witness, Do not defraud, Honour your

father and mother." ' 20 And he said to him, 'Teacher, all these I have observed from my youth.' 21 And Jesus looking upon him loved him, and said to him, 'You lack one thing, go, sell what you have, and give to the poor, and you will have treasure in heaven; and come, follow me.' 22 At that saying his countenance fell, and he went away sorrowful; for he had great possessions.

10:17 *As he was setting out on his journey, a man ran up* i.e. the man came in haste to catch him before he left and 'longing to be in conversation with Christ' (H). Note, Mark says just 'a man' of indeterminate age and quality. It is Matthew (19:20) who made him 'a young man', and Luke (18:18) who made him 'a ruler': hence 'the rich young ruler'. But Mark's is the original, unembellished form of the story. Many have (vainly) speculated about the man's identity: suggestions have included John Mark, Lazarus, Matthias and the beloved disciple. *Good teacher, what must I do to inherit eternal life?* 'inherit eternal life' = 'receive the kingdom of God' (v. 15).

10:18 *Jesus said to him, 'Why do you call me good? No one is good but God alone.'* In Greek it was usual enough to address someone as 'good', but it was contrary to Jewish convention and was almost tantamount to addressing someone as 'holy' or 'divine'. Jesus deprecates the man's flattering words and gestures. He was altogether too obsequious and effusive. Jesus says in effect, 'Don't fling this fulsome title about so casually'. But from early days this verse was found to be puzzling, since on the face of it Jesus seemed to be denying that he was a good man. Matthew (19:17) therefore evaded the difficulty by changing the wording of Jesus's question.

10:19 *You know the commandments* Jesus appears to imply that in order to 'inherit eternal life' a man must keep the commandments, which is very different from what he has said in v. 15, namely that eternal life or the kingdom of God must be received as a free gift. Thus there

is an apparent contradiction. Shakespeare alludes to it in
King Richard II where he makes the king say:

> Thoughts of things divine are intermixed
> . . . and do set the Word itself against the Word.
> As thus: 'Come, little ones'; and then again –
> 'It is as hard to come, as for a camel
> to thread the postern of a needle's eye.'

But we shall see that the contrast is relieved in what follows. *Do not defraud* Some take this to be a summary of
the ninth and tenth commandments, but Jesus did not
specify the *ten* commandments. There were many others.

10:20 *All these I have observed from my youth.* This
surely implies that the man was at least middle-aged. The
reply is complacent: only superficially could anyone observe all the commandments. 'Ignorance of the extent and
spiritual nature of the divine law makes people think themselves in a better condition than they are' (H).

10:21 *Jesus looking upon him loved him* 'Loved' here
could mean 'liked', or 'looked upon him with admiring
affection', or possibly 'caressed him'. N.E.B. translates:
'Jesus looked straight at him; his heart warmed to him.'
Matthew and Luke omit the expression. 'He expressed love
with the earnest look, and as it were smiling expression, of
his eyes' (Be). But is anyone in the Bible ever said to smile?
You lack one thing 'Generally speaking, to men . . . there is
wanting some one thing, this or that; and by the want of
that one thing they are kept back from Christ' (Be). *Go,
sell what you have* Jesus did not make this demand on all
his followers, but 'saw in his conversation with this man
both his possibilities and at the same time the way in
which his wealth and possessions bound him to a conventional goodness' (Br). He needed to make a complete
break and a new beginning.

10:22 *At that saying his countenance fell, and he went
away sorrowful* The idea of completely renouncing his
possessions and way of life in order to adopt the itinerant

existence of Jesus did not attract him. 'Nothing is said about his losing salvation; the N.T. always avoids expressing any "verdicts of damnation".' (Sch). He was sorry to find that eternal life could be had only at such a price and we are not told that he returned, though it has been well said that he came back centuries later in the person of Francis of Assisi.

23 And Jesus looked around and said to his disciples, 'How hard it will be for those who have riches to enter the kingdom of God!' 24 And the disciples were amazed at his words. But Jesus said to them again, 'Children, how hard it is to enter the kingdom of God! 25 It is easier for a camel to go through the eye of a needle than for a rich man to enter the kingdom of God.' 26 And they were exceedingly astonished, and said to him, 'Then who can be saved?' 27 Jesus looked at them and said, 'With men it is impossible, but not with God; for all things are possible with God.' 28 Peter began to say to him, 'Lo, we have left everything, and followed you.' 29 Jesus said, 'Truly, I say to you, there is no one who has left house or brothers or sisters or mother or father or children or lands, for my sake and for the gospel, 30 who will not receive a hundredfold now in this time, houses and brothers and sisters and mothers and children and lands, with persecutions, and in the age to come eternal life. 31 But many that are first will be last, and the last first.'

10:23 *How hard it will be for those who have riches* 'How hard'=with what difficulty. The rich man is to be pitied because of his great temptations, which too easily give him a false sense of security. 'There is an almost forgotten saying of Jesus, "How hard it is for the rich to enter into the kingdom of God!" The Church does not preach it, least of all that portion of the Church which holds most strongly by verbal inspiration. The various branches of the Church seem to agree that Jesus was mistaken here, for they choose men with this handicap for high and representative office and listen to their advice with deference' (Frank Lenwood).

10:24 *How hard it is to enter the kingdom of God!* A.V. 'for them that trust in riches' is an early gloss that was designed to tone down what Jesus had just said. It is specially hard for the rich, but hard indeed for anyone, to enter the kingdom of God.

10:25 *It is easier for a camel to go through the eye of a needle* – a characteristic oriental hyperbole. 'An elephant through the eye of a needle' seems to have been a proverbial Jewish expression. Attempts to weaken the expression by saying that 'camel' is a misreading for 'rope', and that there was a postern gate in Jerusalem known as 'the needle's eye', are uncalled for.

10:26f. *Then who can be saved?* ' "If this were the case," they say, "no one would ever attain salvation" . . . "Quite right," Jesus replies, "no one ever does on the basis of human effort; if men *are* saved, it is solely due to the grace and unlimited power of God" ' (N). This is Paul's teaching that man is justified by grace and faith alone.

10:28-31 These were detached sayings that Mark thought could appropriately be added here.

10:28 *Lo, we have left everything* The *we* is emphatic. Did Peter mean by *we* himself and his brother Andrew, or all the disciples? 'We have done,' he says, 'what the rich man refused to do: how will it be with us?'

10:29 A.V. has *or wife* (derived from Luke 18:29), but does not have 'or wives' in v. 30, for good reason! Those of the apostles who were married may have kept their wives.

10:30 *A hundredfold now in this time* They will receive a twofold recompense in this age, the advantages derived from belonging to the Christian community which makes houses and other possessions available to all and provides family relationships in the Church; and in the age to come eternal life. *With persecutions* is an awkward addition by an early editor or copyist.

10:31 *Many that are first will be last, and the last first* This was an isolated, perhaps a proverbial, saying, for which each evangelist provided a different setting: see Matthew 20:16; Luke 13:30. Mark will have regarded it either as an encouragement or as a warning to the disciples.

32 And they were on the road, going up to Jerusalem, and Jesus was walking ahead of them; and they were amazed, and those who followed were afraid. And taking the twelve again, he began to tell them what was to happen to him, 33 saying, 'Behold, we are going up to Jerusalem; and the Son of man will be delivered to the chief priests and the scribes, and they will condemn him to death, and deliver him to the Gentiles; 34 and they will mock him, and spit upon him, and scourge him, and kill him, and after three days he will rise.'

10:32 *Jesus was walking ahead of them* 'leading the way' (N.E.B.). Of this verse Rudolf Otto wrote: 'This passage renders with supreme simplicity and force the immediate impression of the numinous (i.e. transcendent mystery) that issued from the man Jesus, and no artistry of characterization could do it so powerfully as these few masterly and pregnant words.' Mark here implies that the disciples realized the gravity of the situation.

10:33f. This is the third prediction of the Passion (see 8:31; 9:30). It is the most detailed, and has no doubt been influenced by Mark's narrative of the Passion in chapters 14 and 15.

35 And James and John, the sons of Zebedee, came forward to him, and said to him, 'Teacher, we want you to do for us whatever we ask of you.' 36 And he said to them, 'What do you want me to do for you?' 37 And they said to him, 'Grant us to sit, one at your right hand and one at your left, in your glory.' 38 But Jesus said to them, 'You do not know what you are asking.

Are you able to drink the cup that I drink, or to be baptized with the baptism with which I am baptized?' 39 And they said to him, 'We are able.' And Jesus said to them, 'The cup that I drink you will drink; and with the baptism with which I am baptized, you will be baptized; 40 but to sit at my right hand or at my left is not mine to grant, but it is for those for whom it has been prepared.' 41 And when the ten heard it, they began to be indignant at James and John. 42 And Jesus called them to him, and said to them, 'You know that those who are supposed to rule over the Gentiles lord it over them, and their great men exercise authority over them. 43 But it shall not be so among you; but whoever would be great among you must be your servant, 44 and whoever would be first among you must be slave of all. 45 For the Son of man also came not to be served but to serve, and to give his life as a ransom for many.'

10:35 *James and John . . . came forward to him* The question they are going to ask reflects no credit on them. That presumably is why Matthew (20:20) makes their mother ask it on their behalf.

10:37 *One at your right hand and one at your left* i.e. the places of honour, possibly the chief seats at the messianic banquet (cp. note on 6:34).

10:38 *Are you able to drink the cup that I drink . . .?* In the Old Testament 'the cup' is frequently a symbol of suffering; see e.g. Ezekiel 23:31-34. *Or to be baptized with the baptism with which I am baptized?* Likewise being submerged in water as in baptism is a metaphor for suffering; see e.g. Psalm 69:1f.

10.39 *The cup that I drink you will drink* This is a prediction that James and John will be martyred, and it is to be presumed that the prediction had been fulfilled before the gospel was written, else it would have called for comment. The martyrdom of James is recorded in Acts (12:2) and, despite the later tradition that John lived to a great age, there is some evidence that he too was martyred about the same time. The matter is naturally discussed in commentaries on the fourth gospel.

10:40 *To sit at my right hand or at my left is not mine to grant* 'The Lord disclaims the right to dispose in an arbitrary manner of the higher rewards of the Kingdom' (Sw). They are not casual gifts, externally conferred, but come of God's decree to those who are qualified by faith.

10:41ff. These verses relate to pre-eminence in this age, rather than in the age to come. *When the ten heard it, they began to be indignant at James and John* 'These discovered their own ambition, in their displeasure at the ambition of James and John; and Christ took this occasion to warn them against it, and all their successors in the ministry of the gospel' (H). *Those who are supposed to rule over the Gentiles* But surely they *did* rule. Perhaps this is ironical. Other possible translations are: 'Those who aspire to rule' or 'The recognized rulers' (N.E.B.). Mark had seen plenty of the seamier side of Roman imperial rule in Nero's Rome. *Their great men exercise authority over them* This seems to be a weak statement. Other translations are: 'Their great men have absolute power' (P); 'Their great men make them feel the weight of their authority' (N.E.B.); 'Their great men tyrannize over them' (Go). *But it shall not be so among you* Are ecclesiastical hierarchies warranted by this standard?

10:45 *To give his life as a ransom for many* There is a large literature about this text because of its bearing on the doctrine of the atonement, but too much dependence should not be placed on a single text. It is generally agreed that *for many* does not exclude its being 'for all' (cp. note on 14:24). The idea of 'ransom' was familiar from the Old Testament. See, especially, 2 Maccabees 7:37f., which concerns the martyrdom of one of the seven brothers.

46 And they came to Jericho; and as he was leaving Jericho with his disciples and a great multitude, Bartimaeus, a blind beggar, the son of Timæus, was sitting

by the roadside. 47 And when he heard that it was Jesus of Nazareth, he began to cry out and say, 'Jesus, Son of David, have mercy on me!' 48 And many rebuked him, telling him to be silent; but he cried out all the more, 'Son of David, have mercy on me!' 49 And Jesus stopped and said, 'Call him.' And they called the blind man, saying to him, 'Take heart; rise, he is calling you.' 50 And throwing off his mantle he sprang up and came to Jesus. 51 And Jesus said to him, 'What do you want me to do for you?' And the blind man said to him, 'Master, let me receive my sight.' 52 And Jesus said to him, 'Go your way; your faith has made you well.' And immediately he received his sight and followed him on the way.

10:46 *Jericho* in the Jordan valley was fifteen miles north-east of Jerusalem. *Bar-Timaeus* means 'son of Timaeus'. The wording is curious. *A blind beggar* 'The numerous diseases of the eyes in the East had little prospect of cure in those days, and the lot of those afflicted by them was harsh. There was nothing for most of them but to beg' (Sch).

10:47 *Jesus of Nazareth,* to distinguish him from others who bore the same name. *Jesus, Son of David* In view of the expectation that the Messiah would be descended from David, this must be regarded as a messianic title. It is the first time that Jesus's messiahship is publicly acknowledged in Mark.

10:50 *Throwing off his mantle* The beggar flings aside his cloak in order to run more quickly, signifying the alacrity with which the call of Jesus should always be answered. *He sprang up and came to Jesus* His blindness was not apparently total, else he could not have approached Jesus without help.

10:52 *Has made you well* The Greek word can denote both healing and salvation. *And followed him on the way —* along the road to Jerusalem or in the way of Christian discipleship or are both implied?

112

11 : 1 And when they drew near to Jerusalem, to Bethphage and Bethany, at the Mount of Olives, he sent two
of his disciples, 2 and said to them, 'Go into the village
opposite you, and immediately as you enter it you will
find a colt tied, on which no one has ever sat; untie it and
bring it. 3 If anyone says to you, "Why are you doing
this?" say, "The Lord has need of it and will send it
back here immediately".' 4 And they went away, and
found a colt tied at the door out in the open street; and
they untied it. 5 And those who stood there said to
them, 'What are you doing, untying the colt?' 6 And
they told them what Jesus had said; and they let them
go. 7 And they brought the colt to Jesus, and threw
their garments on it; and he sat upon it. 8 And many
spread their garments on the road, and others spread
leafy branches which they had cut from the fields. 9 And
those who went before and those who followed cried
out, 'Hosanna! Blessed is he who comes in the name
of the Lord! 10 Blessed is the kingdom of our father
David that is coming! Hosanna in the highest!'

This is often described as the *triumphal* entry into Jerusalem, but the epithet derives from what is said in the other
gospels. Mark's account is much more restrained than
theirs and no doubt rightly so, for if Jesus had entered
the city obviously as Messiah and been openly acclaimed
as such he would surely have been arrested at once by
the Jewish authorities. Mark, it seems, saw it as a *veiled*
messianic entry in accordance with his theory of the
messianic secret. He surely had in mind, although he does
not quote it, the prophecy of Zechariah 9 : 9, and this may
have been in the mind of Jesus and his immediate disciples. Jesus chose to enter the city in a manner that would
signify his messiahship to those who could understand,
while concealing it from the rest. There may indeed have
been a spontaneous outburst of enthusiasm from a small
group of pilgrims which later could have been exaggerated.
M. Henry justly observes that Jesus 'did not steal into the

city incognito, as one that durst not show his face'.

11:1 *When they drew near to Jerusalem, to Bethphage and Bethany* As before, Mark is ill-informed about the topography. Bethphage is nearer to the city than Bethany, but it is possible that one of the names should be omitted. *At the Mount of Olives* which was associated with the expected coming of the Messiah, see Zechariah 14:4.

11:2 *You will find a colt tied* This would hardly be an unusual sight in a Jewish village. It is implied that Jesus had supernatural knowledge about the location of the colt. This may be an embellishment of the original version of the story. *On which no one has ever sat* It was a common idea in antiquity that anything intended for sacred or ceremonial use should not have been used before for secular purposes, e.g. see Numbers 19:2; 1 Samuel 6:7.

11:3 *The Lord has need of it* 'The Lord' here may mean God or the owner of the colt, though several modern translators have 'The Master needs it'. 'This colt was borrowed . . . Christ went upon the water in a borrowed boat, ate the passover in a borrowed chamber, was buried in a borrowed sepulchre, and here rode on a borrowed ass. Let not Christians scorn to be beholden one to another, and, when need is, to go a-borrowing' (H).

11:7 *Threw their garments on it* instead of a saddle.

11:8 *Many spread their garments on the road* as a spontaneous sign of respect, cp. 2 Kings 9:13, and the modern practice of putting down the red carpet. *Leafy branches* cp. 1 Maccabees 13:51. It has been reasonably conjectured that originally this story was associated not with the feast of Passover but with the feast of Dedication, when as at the feast of Tabernacles green branches, which were known as 'hosannas', were carried by the people. There are good grounds for supposing that Jesus came to Jerusalem more than a week before his death, and indeed that he had visited the city previously, as the fourth gospel says. What Mark narrates in these chapters could hardly be fitted in to the very limited time that he allows.

11:9f. These verses echo Psalm 118:25f. where in

Hebrew the word *Hosanna* (which means 'save now') comes. This was one of the Hallel Psalms that were recited at the feast. Mark thinks of the crowd as rendering unconscious homage to the Messiah.

11 And he entered Jerusalem, and went into the temple; and when he had looked round at everything, as it was already late, he went out to Bethany with the twelve.

11:11 *When he had looked round at everything* Not of course as a sightseer, but in order to take stock of the scene where he was going to take action on the morrow. Matthew and Luke present the course of events differently.

12 On the following day, when they came from Bethany, he was hungry. 13 And seeing in the distance a fig tree in leaf, he went to see if he could find anything on it. When he came to it, he found nothing but leaves, for it was not the season for figs. 14 And he said to it, 'May no one ever eat fruit from you again.' And his disciples heard it.

This strange story (see the sequel in v. 20) of the cursing of the fig tree resembles the bizarre miracles that are a feature of the apocryphal gospels. It seems incredible that Jesus would not know the season for figs, though we may note that Archbishop Carrington says 'there are many kinds of fig tree in Palestine, and some do bear figs at Passover even though that is not "the season of figs"; I have seen a photograph of branches loaded with figs at this time.' Anyhow, why should Jesus curse the tree? Various suggestions have been made to meet the difficulty: that a parable about a fig tree (such as that in Luke 13:6-9) has somehow been transformed into a miracle story; that there was a withered tree on the road between Bethany and Jerusalem which gave rise to this story; or that a story about a tree that had a fine show of leaves but no fruit, which was used to make the point that Judaism with its fine show of rites and ceremonies but without the fruits of righteousness would suffer a fate like this, has here taken material form. There are passages in the Old Testament which suggest this last idea: see Jeremiah 8:13; Ezekiel 17:24. Without some such explanation, it seems to be a senseless miracle, quite uncharacteristic of Jesus.

15 And they came to Jerusalem. And he entered the temple and began to drive out those who sold and those who bought in the temple, and he overturned the tables of the money-changers and the seats of those who sold pigeons; 16 and he would not allow any one to carry anything through the temple. 17 And he taught, and said to them, 'Is it not written, "My house shall be called a house of prayer for all the nations"? But you have made it a den of robbers.' 18 And the chief priests and the scribes heard it and sought a way to destroy him; for they feared him, because all the multitude was astonished at his teaching. 19 And when evening came they went out of the city.

The fourth gospel places the cleansing of the temple at the beginning of our Lord's ministry (see John 2:13-16). It can hardly have happened twice, and the arguments in favour of, and against, the synoptic and Johannine dating of the episode are well balanced. There were Old Testament prophecies that anticipated a cleansing of the temple: see Hosea 9:15; Zechariah 14:21; Malachi 3:1. So the action of Jesus could be understood to have a messianic character.

11:15 *He entered the temple* This was the temple that Herod the Great began to rebuild in 20 B.C. The present incident took place in the Court of the Gentiles. *Those who sold and those who bought in the temple* The sale of what was required for sacrifice was an obvious convenience for pilgrims. Animals had to be inspected and certified as

116

ceremonially 'clean'. *He overturned the tables of the money-changers* Temple dues had to be paid in Tyrian coinage, so that Greek or Roman money had to be changed into that. This also was a convenience for pilgrims. It is not clear who derived profit from this business, but no doubt the priests had a lively interest in it.

11:16 *He would not allow any one to carry anything through the temple* Mark alone mentions this. Jesus may have been invoking an old regulation which was being disregarded by those who used the temple precincts as a short cut. In general, Jesus seems to have been protesting dramatically against the secularization of a place that should have been kept holy for worship and as free as possible from disturbance. In the light of this, is the buying and selling that now goes on in our cathedrals and churches tolerable?

11:17 *My house shall be called a house of prayer for all the nations* This is a quotation from Isaiah 56:7. The Lord's action was on behalf of the Gentiles who were being deprived of their rights in the temple. *But you have made it a den of robbers* Cp. Jeremiah 7:11; but the passage in Jeremiah 'does not necessarily imply extortion on the part of the merchants' (Gr). 'But you have turned it into a thieves' kitchen' (P).

11:18 This explains why the Jewish authorities did not take action at once.

20 As they passed by in the morning, they saw the fig tree withered away to its roots. 21 And Peter remembered and said to him, 'Master, look! The fig tree which you cursed has withered.' 22 And Jesus answered them, 'Have faith in God. 23 Truly, I say to you, whoever says to this mountain, "Be taken up and cast into the sea", and does not doubt in his heart, but believes that what he says will come to pass, it will be done for him. 24 Therefore I tell you, whatever you ask in prayer, believe that you have received it, and it will be yours. 25 And whenever you stand praying, forgive, if you have

anything against any one; so that your Father also who is in heaven may forgive you your trespasses.'

11:20f. See note on vv. 12ff.

11:22-26 Mark uses the fig tree incident as a peg on which to hang some detached sayings about faith and prayer. There is no logical connection between them.

11:22 *Have faith in God* This seems a platitude by itself, but in its original context it no doubt had an incisive point.

11:23 *Whoever says to this mountain* This is most likely to have been spoken by the sea of Tiberias in Galilee, though it is said that the Dead Sea can be seen from the Mount of Olives. Removing mountains was a metaphor for doing things of great difficulty: cp. Zechariah 4:7. This is a hyperbolic way of saying that through faith God can enable men to do what seems absurd or impossible. Is this more difficult to believe now than in the time of Christ, or do instances of it still abound?

11:24 *Whatever you ask in prayer, believe that you have received it* In other words, no limits should be set to the power of prayer.

11:25 *Whenever you stand praying, forgive* Standing was a normal posture for prayer. The vulgar idea that 'Let us pray' means 'Let us kneel down' needs to be corrected. This verse is reminiscent of the Lord's Prayer which Mark does not record, though he was obviously familiar with it. Verse 26 is not in the best manuscripts and is rightly omitted by R.S.V.

27 And they came again to Jerusalem. And as he was walking in the temple, the chief priests and the scribes and the elders came to him, 28 and they said to him, 'By what authority are you doing these things, or who gave you this authority to do them?' 29 Jesus said to them, 'I will ask you a question; answer me, and I will tell you by what authority I do these things. 30 Was the baptism of John from heaven or from men? Answer me.' 31

And they argued with one another, 'If we say, "From heaven,' he will say, 'Why then did you not believe him?" 32 But shall we say, "From men"?' – they were afraid of the people, for all held that John was a real prophet. 33 So they answered Jesus, 'We do not know.' And Jesus said to them, 'Neither will I tell you by what authority I do these things.'

Mark now gives us a series of conflict stories. Some of them may have belonged to other occasions, but the first is fittingly placed after the cleansing of the Temple which would certainly have provoked the question that is put to Jesus.

11:27 *As he was walking in the temple* 'The Peripatetic philosophers were so called from the custom they had of walking when they taught' (H). *The chief priests and the scribes and the elders came to him* This was evidently a deputation from the Sanhedrin, which was the supreme council and highest court of justice at Jerusalem. Those three classes of people were its members: *the chief priests* being the hierarchy that was directly responsible for the Temple; *the scribes*, later knowns as rabbis, the accredited teachers of the Jewish religion; *the elders*, i.e. other members of the Sanhedrin like Nicodemus and Joseph of Arimathea.

11:29 *Jesus said to them, 'I will ask you a question'* To ask a counter-question was a common gambit in rabbinic discussions (cp. 10:3).

11:30 *The baptism of John* which is meant to include his whole activity and mission. *From heaven* i.e. from God. The Jews frequently spoke of heaven in order to avoid mentioning the divine name.

11:33 The implication is of course that Jesus like John derived his authority from God. As Chrysostom remarked, Jesus did not say, 'I do not know', but 'I do not tell'. 'They did not deserve to be told, who, it was plain, did not contend for truth, but victory' (H). Would Christian apologists today be well advised, when asked questions, to adopt this apparently evasive, but really thought-provoking, method of reply, instead of trying to give direct answers?

12:1 And he began to speak to them in parables. 'A man planted a vineyard, and set a hedge around it, and dug a pit for the wine press, and built a tower, and let it out to tenants, and went into another country. 2 When the time came, he sent a servant to the tenants, to get from them some of the fruit of the vineyard. 3 And they took him and beat him, and sent him away empty-handed. 4 Again he sent to them another servant, and they wounded him in the head, and treated him shamefully. 5 And he sent another, and him they killed; and so with many others, some they beat and some they killed. 6 He had still one other, a beloved son; finally he sent him to them, saying, "They will respect my son." 7 But those tenants said to one another, "This is the heir; come, let us kill him, and the inheritance will be ours.' 8 And they took him and killed him, and cast him out of the vineyard. 9 What will the owner of the vineyard do? He will come and destroy the tenants, and give the vineyard to others. 10 Have you not read this scripture:

"The very stone which the builders rejected
    has become the head of the corner;
11   this was the Lord's doing,
  and it is marvellous in our eyes"?'

12 And they tried to arrest him, but feared the multitude, for they perceived that he had told the parable against them; so they left him and went away.

12:1 *He began to speak to them in parables* But there is only one here. Either this expression originally introduced a series of parables of which Mark has retained only one, or *in parables* here means 'parabolically'. In any case this story of the wicked tenants is quite unlike Jesus's normal parables, which were not allegories as this is (see note on 4:1-9), but stories designed to illustrate one point. Moreover, they were taken from real life, whereas this is quite imaginary and extremely improbable as a story. What may have happened is that a story told or used by Jesus as a parable was transformed by the early Church into an elaborate allegory for use in controversy with the Jews. In the allegory the vineyard is Israel, the owner is God, the tenants the Jewish authorities, the servants the Old Testament prophets, and the son and heir Jesus. *A man planted a vineyard* Israel was often likened to a vineyard, e.g. see Isaiah 5:1f. Palestinian vineyards were surrounded by *a hedge* or wall to afford protection from wild animals; they had *a pit for the wine press* which may have been hewn out of solid rock; *a tower* that would be used as a storeroom and a look-out place against jackals or thieves: cp. Song of Songs 2:15.

12:2 *When the time came* This would be in the fifth year, see Leviticus 19:23ff.

12:4 *They wounded him in the head* This is probably correct, but some think 'beheaded' would be a more accurate translation.

12:7 *This is the heir; come, let us kill him, and the inheritance will be ours* Limited as the logic of criminals often is, that of the tenants is incredible. But from the point of view of the allegory those who delivered Jesus to death thought they were assuring for themselves alone the control of the salvation revealed in the Law, from which those whom Jesus has called would be excluded. They wanted to confiscate for their own benefit the heavenly Father's inheritance.

12:8 *Cast him out of the vineyard* i.e. left him unburied, which was a final outrage.

12:9 *What will the owner ... do?* The allegorical meaning is that God, who has for so long delayed the manifestation of justice, will chastise the Jews and destroy Jerusalem. Archbishop Carrington commented: 'The tenants are a recognizable portrait of the Jerusalem priesthood, and a warning to all priesthoods, and all bishops and archbishops and presidents and principals and administrators who forget that they are only tenants of their office at God's pleasure, and act as if the vineyard belonged to them.' When bishops talk about *my* diocese and priests about *my* parish, are they speaking as they should?

12:10f. The quotation from Psalm 118:22f. was a favourite one in the early Church and occurs several times in the New Testament. *The head of the corner* – either the corner-stone that holds the walls of the building together or the keystone of the arch or gateway.

13 And they sent to him some of the Pharisees and some of the Herodians, to entrap him in his talk. 14 And they came and said to him, 'Teacher, we know that you are true, and care for no man; for you do not regard the position of men, but truly teach the way of God. Is it lawful to pay taxes to Caesar, or not? 15 Should we pay them, or should we not?' But knowing their hypocrisy, he said to them, 'Why put me to the test? Bring me a coin, and let me look at it.' 16 And they brought one. And he said to them, 'Whose likeness and inscription is this?' They said to him, 'Caesar's.' 17 Jesus said to them, 'Render to Caesar the things that are Caesar's, and to God the things that are God's.' And they were amazed at him.

The poll-tax which was paid direct into the imperial treasury was naturally unpopular with the Jews, since it was a sign of their national subjection to Rome. The question was cleverly contrived: if Jesus gave an affirmative answer he would disgust the people, whereas a negative answer would make him liable to be denounced to the Romans.

12:13 *Some of the Pharisees and some of the Herodians* The Pharisees were of course against the tax, but the Herodians (supporters of Herod Antipas, who would have come to Jerusalem from Galilee for the feast) depended upon Roman favour and so would have acquiesced in the payment of the tax.

12:14 The challenge to Jesus is preceded by some fulsome, hypocritical compliments. *Is it lawful to pay taxes to Caesar?* This head tax had been payable by the inhabitants of Judea since A.D. 6, when Herod Archelaus had been deposed and Roman procurators took over the administration of the country. The tax was paid with a silver denarius which bore a relief of the emperor's head.

12:6 *Whose likeness and inscription is this?* According to ancient ideas coins ultimately belonged to the ruler who issued them and whose image they bore. So Jesus is saying that the money they have is Caesar's and therefore they implicitly acknowledge his authority.

12:7 *Render to Caesar the things that are Caesar's, and to God the things that are God's.* 'To pay tribute to Caesar was not much, a denarius a year, and the coin belonged to Caesar anyway – let him have it back! But to pay tribute to God, to render him his due, to pay the things that belonged to God – duty, service, obedience, worship – this was everything, and the whole of life' (Gr). This would have been an important message for Mark's readers in Rome. *They were amazed at him* – at his skill in evading the trap that had been set for him, or at the profound truth of what he said?

18 And Sadducees came to him, who say that there is no resurrection; and they asked him a question, saying, 19 'Teacher, Moses wrote for us that if a man's brother dies and leaves a wife, but leaves no child, the man must take the wife, and raise up children for his brother. 20 There were seven brothers; the first took a wife, and when he died left no children; 21 and the second took her, and died, leaving no children; and the third likewise; 22 and the seven left no children. Last of all the woman also died. 23 In the resurrection whose wife will she be? For the seven had her as wife.' 24 Jesus said to them, 'Is not this why you are wrong, that you know neither the scriptures nor the power of God? 25 For

when they rise from the dead, they neither marry nor
are given in marriage, but are like angels in heaven.
26 And as for the dead being raised, have you not read
in the book of Moses, in the passage about the bush, how
God said to him, "I am the God of Abraham, and the
God of Isaac, and the God of Jacob"? 27 He is not God
of the dead, but of the living; you are quite wrong.'

This is another conflict story, arising out of a question
asked by the Sadducees who are here mentioned for the
first – and last – time by Mark. The origin of the name is
obscure. They were the aristocratic party to which many
of the priests belonged. They were worldly and wealthy.
They were conservative in doctrine and opposed to the
innovations of the Pharisees as well as to the strictness of
their piety. In particular, they rejected belief in the resurrection of the dead which was a tenet of pharisaic doctrine.
They appealed to the Torah (Law) and deplored traditional
developments. They might be described as 'low church'
and Erastian.

12:19 *Teacher, Moses wrote for us* This was known as
the levirate marriage: see Deuteronomy 25:5-10. The main
object of the ordinance had been to keep the possession of
property within the family. The word 'levirate' has nothing
to do with 'Levi', but is derived from the Latin word *levir*,
which means 'husband's brother'. Although in the time of
Christ this ordinance had fallen into disuse, the Sadducees
took advantage of it to propound a theoretical or hypo-
thetical question, based on a logical possibility. It is the
kind of question that ingenious and sophisticated minds
like to fabricate. The purpose was to show that belief in
the resurrection issues in absurdity.

12:20 *There were seven brothers* The number seven is
conventional in stories of this kind: cp. Tobit 3:7f.

12:22 *The seven left no children* If the last brother had
had a son by the woman, he would have been the preferred
husband.

12:24 *You know neither the scriptures* Jesus's reply is

very effective as against the Sadducees. In v. 26 he is going to quote from the Pentateuch (Exodus 3:6) which was the part of the scripture which they regarded as the final authority. *Nor the power of God* 'They could not but know that God is almighty, but they would not apply that doctrine to the matter' (H).

12:25 But first he points out that the conditions of the after-life are quite different from those of this life. *They neither marry nor are given in marriage* i.e. men do not marry, and women are not given in marriage, which was the matrimonial convention in those days. *But are like angels in heaven* Acts 23:8 says that the Sadducees did not believe in angels but this cannot be correct, since there are plenty of references to them in the Pentateuch. The Jews recognized the sexless nature of angels: e.g. in 1 Enoch 5:6f. we read: 'You are everliving spirits . . . therefore I have not created wives for you.' 'Turks and infidels expect sensual pleasures in their fools' paradises, but Christians know better things, that flesh and blood shall not inherit the kingdom of God' (H).

12:26 *In the passage about the bush* (i.e. the burning bush in Exodus 3:1-6). The Old Testament was not at that time divided into chapters and verses, but one could refer to a paragraph in the Bible. Cp. Romans 11:2, where N.E.B. rightly translates: 'in the story of Elijah' and Moffat: 'in the passage called "Elijah".' The point of the quotation from Exodus (which may strike us as a purely verbal one) is that God said *I am the God of Abraham* etc. at a time when they were no longer alive on earth; therefore they must have been alive in the resurrection state. In other words, the Torah itself, which the Sadducees so highly esteemed, postulated belief in the resurrection of the dead.

28 And one of the scribes came up and heard them disputing with one another, and seeing that he answered them well, asked him, 'Which commandment is the first of all?' 29 Jesus answered, 'The first is, "Hear, O Israel:

The Lord our God, the Lord is one; 30 and you shall love the Lord your God with all your heart, and with all your strength." 31 The second is this, "You shall love your neighbour as yourself." There is no other commandment greater than these.' 32 And the scribe said to him, 'You are right, Teacher; you have truly said that he is one, and that there is no other but he; 33 and to love him with all the heart, and with all the understanding, and with all the strength, and to love one's neighbour as oneself, is much more than all whole burnt offerings and sacrifices.' 34 And when Jesus saw that he answered wisely, he said to him, 'You are not far from the kingdom of God.' And after that no one dared to ask him any question.

The scribe, who now puts a question to Jesus, does so in a friendly spirit. In Matthew (22:34-40) and Luke (10:25-28; 20:39f.) it is otherwise. Indeed Luke's version is so different that it may refer to another occasion. Perhaps Mark placed the incident here in order to show that, despite the conflict between Jesus and the Jewish authorities, he was fundamentally orthodox in his allegiance to the Torah.

12:28 *Which commandment is the first of all?* This was a question that was discussed by the rabbis, i.e. whether there was one commandment that was basic to all the rest. The famous rabbi Hillel, when told by a Gentile that he would become a proselyte if he were taught the whole Law while the rabbi stood on one foot, replied: 'What you hate for yourself, do not do to your neighbour: this is the whole Law, the rest is commentary.' 'Some rabbis held that the first commandment was the one given to Adam – to increase and multiply and beget children' (Ca).

12:29ff. The answer of Jesus combines two texts from the Torah. Deuteronomy 6:4f. about the love of God, and Leviticus 19:18 about love of the neighbour. The former is known as the *Shema* (Hebrew for 'hear') which every pious Jew recites daily. It is not certain whether anyone

126

before Jesus had brought these two commandments together in this way. *Your neighbour* here means 'your fellow Israelite'. Jesus elsewhere extended the meaning, as in the parable of the Good Samaritan.

12:33 *More than all whole burnt offerings and sacrifices* cp. 1 Samuel 15:22; Hosea 6:6.

12:34a *You are not far from the kingdom of God* 'You come near to possessing the dispositions needed for entry into the kingdom.'

12:34b *And after that no one dared to ask him any question* This would come more naturally after v. 27 and perhaps somehow got displaced. Alternatively, one must say that 'the way in which our Lord dealt with this friendly enquirer . . . produced such an impression of religious awe upon the bystanders that no one after that ventured any more to take the initiative in questioning him' (R).

35 And as Jesus taught in the temple, he said, 'How can the scribes say that the Christ is the son of David? 36 David himself, inspired by the Holy Spirit, declared,

> "The Lord said to my Lord,
>   Sit at my right hand,
>   till I put thy enemies under thy feet."

37 David himself calls him Lord; so how is he his son?' And the great throng heard him gladly.

In this puzzling passage, Jesus appears at first sight to be denying the Davidic descent of the Messiah, but this can hardly be so, since everywhere else in the New Testament it is affirmed in one way or another, and Mark himself has testified to it in 10:47f. Probably the point being made is that the Messiah is much more than a son of David: he is the Son of God. Mark certainly held that to be so, but is it consistent with his theory of the messianic secret that Jesus should be taking an initiative in teaching about this? Another suggestion is that we have here only the concluding part of a conflict story. It is difficult to understand because the first part is missing. It is quite likely that this is a fragment of a discussion from early Christian questioning about messiahship. Other references to Psalm 110 in the New Testament show that much interest was taken in it in the early Church, though it was not till much later apparently that Jews saw messianic significance in it.

12:36 *David himself, inspired by the Holy Spirit* i.e. speaking as a prophet. It is assumed that David was the author of Psalm 110, whereas it is in fact a Maccabean psalm, composed many centuries after the time of David. It used to worry some Christians that Jesus should be represented as accepting the Davidic authorship of the psalm. But as in the case of the Mosaic authorship of the Pentateuch (see 10:6 above), it was a condition of his becoming genuinely human that he should share the opinions about literary and historical matters that were current at the time of his incarnation.

12:37 *And the great throng heard him gladly* This refers to what follows rather than to what has just been said. Other possible translations are: 'Most of the people liked to hear him' (Wi) and 'The great majority of the people heard him with delight' (J).

38 And in his teaching he said, 'Beware of the scribes, who like to go about in long robes, and to have salutations in the market places 39 and the best seats in the synagogues and the places of honour at feasts, 40 who devour widows' houses and for a pretence make long prayers. They will receive the greater condemnation.'

This section follows here because it has to do with scribes. There is no logical connection with what precedes. It is an extract from a much longer discourse, for which see Matthew 23 and Luke 11.

12:38 *The scribes, who like to go about in long robes*

i.e. the Jewish outer garment or cloak, known as the *tallith*, of which the scribes liked to wear a long and flowing fashion. 'Their going in such clothing was not sinful, but their *loving* to go in it, priding themselves in it, valuing themselves in it, commanding respect by it' (H). What about ecclesiastical vestments?

12 : 39 *The best seats in the synagogue* i.e. the bench in front of the ark which contained the scripture, and facing the people. *And the places of honour at feasts* cp. Luke 14 : 7-11.

12 : 40 *Who devour widows' houses* Perhaps 'through unscrupulous acceptance of hospitality and support' (Gr). *And for a pretence make long prayers* 'The point may be that they took large sums from credulous old women as a reward for the prolonged prayers which they professed to make on their behalf' (N).

It must not be supposed that these charges could justly be laid against a majority of the scribes.

41 And he sat down opposite the treasury, and watched the multitude putting money into the treasury. Many rich people put in large sums. 42 And a poor widow came, and put in two copper coins, which make a penny. 43 And he called his disciples to him, and said to them, 'Truly, I say to you, this poor widow has put in more than all those who are contributing to the treasury. 44 For they all contributed out of their abundance; but she out of her poverty has put in everything she had, her whole living.'

In contrast to the bad scribes who devour widows' houses, we have now the tale of the good widow and her sacrifice.

12 : 41 *The treasury* can mean either a room or a receptacle, perhaps the hall in the Temple, named after the chest with trumpet-shaped tubes into which coins were dropped for the support of the Temple worship. This has been called 'the Peter's pence of the Jews'.

129

12:42 *And put in two copper coins* She had only two minute coins left and she gave them both. How did Jesus know that she was a widow and poor, and what other people contributed? Schnackenburg says that 'visitors to the temple did not insert the money themselves as we do into collection boxes, but handed it to the priests who put it in the receptacles as the donor decided. This explains how Jesus could see what the poor widow gave. She named her amount and its purpose to the priest and Jesus would hear her.'

12:44 This saying would be a good lead into the story of the Passion in chapters 14 and 15, when Jesus gave everything he had for mankind. It is possible that chapter 14 originally followed directly, and that chapter 13 was added by the evangelist as an afterthought.

13:1 And as he came out of the temple, one of his disciples said to him, 'Look, Teacher, what wonderful stones and what wonderful buildings!' 2 And Jesus said to him, 'Do you see those great buildings? There will not be left here one stone upon another, that will not be thrown down.' 3 And as he sat on the Mount of Olives opposite the temple, Peter and James and John and Andrew asked him privately, 4 'Tell us, when will this be, and what will be the sign when these things are all to be accomplished?'

This chapter, which is often described as 'The Little Apocalypse', appears to have existed as an independent unit before Mark decided to incorporate it in his gospel; it may not have been an original part of his plan. In this position it has the character of a farewell discourse. In the Old Testament farewell discourses are ascribed to several of the great figures in Israelite history: to Jacob, Moses, Joshua, Samuel and David; and in the New Testament all four gospels ascribe one to Jesus, the one in the fourth gospel most clearly having this character.

As regards the origin of this chapter in Mark, while it

may well contain genuine sayings of Jesus spoken on various occasions, it is, as it stands, a literary composition (to be *read*: see v. 14), the work of an early Christian prophet who spoke in the name of Jesus. He drew on Old Testament prophecy and on the apocalyptic writings that were current at the time. His object, like that of other apocalyptic writers (Daniel, the Revelation of John, etc.) was not so much to provide esoteric information about the future as to strengthen the faith and fidelity of his readers in a time of crisis and uncertainty. This little apocalypse may have originated around A.D. 40 when the Roman emperor Caligula ordered his statue to be set up in the Temple at Jerusalem, but it will have been edited and modified subsequently, as may be inferred from the different forms of this discourse in Matthew and Luke. It would have a powerful message for Mark's readers in Nero's Rome, where there was a great fire as well as persecution, and no one could tell what things were coming to pass on earth.

13:1-4 This is an introduction to the main discourse which runs from v. 5 to v. 27.

13:1 '*Look, Teacher, what wonderful stones and what wonderful buildings!*' The epithet is the same in both cases but it can mean wonderful or great. 'What stupendous stones, what beautiful buildings!' is an alternative translation. Herod's Temple was one of the most splendid buildings of the time. It was built of white marble. Its eastern front was covered with plates of gold which threw back the rays of the rising sun and could be seen for miles around.

13:2 That Jesus did prophesy the destruction of the Temple is confirmed by the fact that this was one of the charges brought against him (see 14:58) and cp. Jeremiah 26:18. In A.D. 70 the Romans burned down and demolished the Temple. News of this may have reached Rome shortly before Mark completed his gospel, and the Christians there would have been much impressed by the fact that their Lord foretold it.

13:3 *As he sat on the Mount of Olives* As we have seen

before, mountains were the proper setting for divine revelations (see note on 9:2).

13:4 *The sign when these things are all to be accomplished* 'These things' at first sight refers to the destruction of the Temple, but as nothing more is said about that in what follows, the reference may be a general one to the signs of the end of all things. But there is an inconsistency in what is going to be said. On the one hand, signs of the end are specified, while, on the other hand, it is said that 'of that day and hour no one knows'. These are two incompatible strains in apocalyptic expectation, which Mark has conjoined without reconciling them. Perhaps one should not look for consistency in such a matter.

5 And Jesus began to say to them, 'Take heed that no one leads you astray. 6 Many will come in my name, saying, "I am he!" and they will lead many astray. 7 And when you hear of wars and rumours of wars, do not be alarmed; this must take place, but the end is not yet. 8 For nation will rise against nation, and kingdom against kingdom; there will be earthquakes in various places, there will be famines; this is but the beginning of the birth-pangs.'

13:5f. *Many will come in my name* This is a warning to beware of false messiahs, of whom a number made their appearance from the time of the Maccabees, e.g. see Acts 5:36f. The most famous was Bar-cochba, leader of a Jewish insurrection in A.D. 132.

13:6f. *When you hear of wars and rumours of wars* Predictions such as these were regular features of Old Testament prophecy and of apocalyptic writing. There were plenty of disasters and ordeals like these during the first century A.D. 2 Thessalonians chapter 2 shows how Christians might be led by such occurrences to think that the coming of the Lord was imminent. *This is but the beginning of the birth-pangs* 'All that is but the beginning of trouble' (M). N.E.B. is nearer to the Greek: 'with these things the birthpangs of the new age begin.' It was part of apocalyptic expectation that the coming of the new age would be preceded by a time of woes, something known as the 'birthpangs of the Messiah'. For the image, cp. Jeremiah 22:23.

9 'But take heed to yourselves; for they will deliver you up to councils; and you will be beaten in synagogues; and you will stand before governors and kings for my sake, to bear testimony before them. 10 And the gospel must first be preached to all nations. 11 And when they bring you to trial and deliver you up, do not be anxious beforehand what you are to say, but say whatever is given you in that hour, for it is not you who speak, but the Holy Spirit. 12 And brother will deliver up brother to death, and the father his child, and children will rise against parents and have them put to death; 13 and you will be hated by all for my name's sake. But he who endures to the end will be saved.'

These verses are a warning to Christians to be prepared for persecution.

13:9 *They will deliver you up to councils* i.e. to local sanhedrins. Mark will have had in mind the experience of Paul and others. *You will stand before governors and kings* This looks like a direct reference to Paul's appearance before Felix, Festus, Herod Agrippa and Caesar's court in Rome. *To bear testimony before them* Witness to the Gospel is borne by prisoners when on trial.

13:10 *And the gospel must first be preached to all nations* This verse seems to be an insertion by Mark or an editor. It breaks the connection between vv. 9 and 11. If Jesus had actually said this, there would not have been the controversy on the subject in the early Church.

13:11 *Do not be anxious beforehand what you are to say* Most of the early Christians were simple folk for whom an appearance in court would be a considerable ordeal, so that these sayings will have spoken very directly

to their condition. In other circumstances they might be
misused as an excuse for lack of preparation.

13:12 *Brother will deliver up brother* Apocalyptic writings often had warnings like these about family divisions.
They will have been a common experience in the first
century, as they have been at many other times; cp. Micah
7:6.

13:13 *You will be hated by all for my name's sake* The
wording will have been affected by Christian experience.
Where and to what extent are Christians hated today? *He
who endures to the end* i.e. he who remains faithful and
holds out to the last.

14 'But when you see the desolating sacrilege set up
where it ought not to be (let the reader understand),
then let those who are in Judea flee to the mountains; 15
let him who is on the housetop not go down, nor enter
his house, to take anything away; 16 and let him who is
in the field not turn back to take his mantle. 17 And
alas for those who are with child and for those who give
suck in those days! 18 Pray that it may not happen in
winter. 19 For in those days there will be such tribulation as has not been from the beginning of the creation
which God created until now, and never will be. 20 And
if the Lord had not shortened the days, no human being
would be saved; but for the sake of the elect, whom he
chose, he shortened the days. 21 And then if any one
says to you, "Look, here is the Christ!" or "Look, there
he is!" do not believe it. 22 False Christs and false
prophets will arise and show signs and wonders, to lead
astray, if possible, the elect. 23 But take heed; I have
told you all things beforehand.'

We are now to be told what will be the signs that the last
days are approaching.

13:14 *When you see the desolating sacrilege* 'The
abomination of desolation' (A.V. and R.V.) is a more
familiar expression. Other translations are: 'the appalling

desecration' (Go), and 'the unmentionable thing'. The expression is derived from Daniel 11:31 where it referred to the profanation of the Temple by Antiochus Epiphanes in 168 B.C. He set up a heathen altar over the altar of burnt-offering (see 1 Maccabees 1:54). We have noticed already that in A.D. 40 the Emperor Caligula made a similar attempt to profane the Temple, and this event will have kept alive the prediction in the book of Daniel. But here the future, not the past, is in view, and the reference is to the expectation that the Anti-Christ would appear before the final coming of the Christ (see 2 Thessalonians 2:3f.). The word translated 'set up' is a masculine participle, and so points to a person rather than a thing.

(*let the reader understand*) This may mean, 'Let the reader note the new and terrible meaning here given to the words of Daniel.' Taylor notes that, whereas in 2 Thessalonians the Temple could be named, it can now be indicated only by the cryptic phrase *where it ought not to be*, and he adds: 'The explanation may well be that, in Rome during a time of persecution, when Christians were crucified and burnt . . ., more precise language was politically dangerous.' *Let those who are in Judea* It is evident that this passage originally had Judea in view, and in point of fact when the Roman armies approached Jerusalem in A.D. 70 the Christians in the city did withdraw to Pella in Perea. For the flight to the mountains, cp. 1 Maccabees 2:27f.

13:15f. These verses point to the need for haste. *Let him who is on the housetop not go down* The roofs of the houses were flat and one could reach the street by an outdoor staircase. *Let him who is in the field* The cloak or outer garment was laid aside for work on the land.

13:17 *Alas for those who are with child* Obviously flight would be especially difficult for nursing or expectant mothers. *And for those who give suck* 'that know not how either to leave the tender infants behind them, or to carry them along with them . . . the time may often be when the greatest comforts may be the greatest burdens' (H).

13:18 *Pray that it may not happen in winter* when the hardships of flight will be grimmer, as multitudes of refugees have found.

13:19 *For in those days there will be such tribulation* This is a quotation from Daniel 12:1.

13:20 *If the Lord had not shortened the days* The biblical faith was that God was in control of history and so he could delay 'the time of the end' and give the wicked further time to repent, or he could hasten it so as to spare the elect the horrors of the final woes.

13:21 *Do not believe it* Ungullibility is a Christian duty, but are Christians as sceptical as they ought to be?

13:22 *False Christs and false prophets* See 2 Thessalonians 2:9f.

13:23 *I have told you You* is emphatic, i.e. the Christian community.

24 'But in those days, after that tribulation, the sun will be darkened, and the moon will not give its light, 25 and the stars will be falling from heaven, and the powers in the heavens will be shaken. 26 And then they will see the Son of man coming in clouds with great power and glory. 27 And then he will send out the angels, and gather his elect from the four winds, from the ends of the earth to the ends of heaven.'

13:24f. The tribulation on earth is followed by celestial portents. Such portents are frequently mentioned in the Old Testament and in apocalyptic writings. 'That this is picture-language, which we must not seek to compress into a literal interpretation, should go without saying' (Cr). But can we be so sure that the ancients did not take it literally?

13:26 *They will see the Son of man coming in clouds* The final consummation, which surely can be spoken of only in figurative or symbolic language, is described in imagery that is derived from Daniel 7:13f. *Then they will see* 'It will be the end of the painful not-seeing which dis-

tinguishes the life of disciples between the Ascension and
the *Parousia*, and throughout which they have to "walk by
faith, not by sight" . . .; and the end of the veiledness which
is the mark both of our Lord's earthly life and of the life
of the Church' (Cr).

13:27 *Then he will send out the angels, and gather his
elect* In Judaism this idea meant the gathering of the Jews
of the dispersion to join the faithful in the holy land: see
e.g. Deuteronomy 30:4; Isaiah 27:12f.; Zechariah 10:8ff.
'Such a gathering of men into a true and lasting brother-
hood has proved to be impossible under the conditions of
Judaism . . ., but would be realized . . . at the *parousia*'
(Sw). *From the ends of the earth to the ends of heaven* A
curious expression: the picture is of the earth as a flat
disc overarched by the vault of heaven. 'They shall be
fetched from one end of the world to the other, so that
none shall be missing from that general assembly' (H).

His elect can be understood exclusively or inclusively.
Christ himself is the Elect of God, the head of the re-
generated human race. All are elect in him, however much
lost in themselves.

13:28-37 This is a supplementary collection of sayings
about watchfulness.

28 'From the fig tree learn its lesson: as soon as its
branch becomes tender and puts forth its leaves, you
know that summer is near. 29 So also, when you see
these things taking place, you know that he is near, at the
very gates. 30 Truly, I say to you, this generation will
not pass away before all these things take place. 31
Heaven and earth will pass away, but my words will not
pass away. 32 But of that day or that hour no one
knows, not even the angels in heaven, nor the Son, but
only the Father. 33 Take heed, watch; for you do not
know when the time will come. 34 It is like a man going
on a journey, when he leaves home and puts his servants
in charge, each with his work, and commands the door-
keeper to be on the watch. 35 Watch therefore – for you

do not know when the master of the house will come, in the evening, or at midnight, or at cockcrow, or in the morning – 36 lest he come suddenly and find you asleep. 37 And what I say to you I say to all: Watch.'

13:29 *When you see these things taking place* 'These things' refers to the signs of the end in general.

13:30 *This generation will not pass away before all these things take place.* The fact that our Lord apparently anticipated that the final consummation would take place in the near future need not be a stumbling-block to faith. 'When the profound realities underlying a situation are depicted in the dramatic form of historical prediction, the certainty and inevitability of the spiritual processes involved are expressed in terms of the immediate imminence of the event' (C. H. Dodd). 'It was, and still is, true to say that the *Parousia* is at hand – and indeed this, so far from being an embarrassing mistake on the part of either Jesus or of the early Church, is an essential part of the Church's faith. Ever since the Incarnation men have been living in the last days' (Cr). The Christian perspective is that of people who are living between the lightning of Christ's first coming and the thunder of his final advent, i.e. with that kind of expectant confidence. Some words of Rudolf Bultmann are relevant here: 'It is a fact that *prophetic consciousness* always expects the judgement of God, and likewise the time of salvation to be brought in by God in the immediate future . . . And the reason this is so is that to the prophetic consciousness the sovereignty of God, the absoluteness of his will, is so overpowering that before it the world sinks away and seems to be at its end.'

13:32 *Of that day or that hour no one knows* This saying has also puzzled Christians who have not realized that 'it is the glory of the Incarnation that Christ accepted those limitations of knowledge which are inseparable from a true humanity' (T).

13:33 *Take heed, watch; for you do not know when the time will come* 'He watches for Christ who has a sensitive, eager, apprehensive mind; who is awake, alive, quick-sighted, zealous in seeking and honouring him; who looks out for him in all that happens, and who would not be surprised, who would not be over-agitated or overwhelmed, if he found that he was coming at once' (J. H. Newman).

13:33-37 These verses say in effect: 'Wait without impatience, but watch and be ready at every moment, for you do not know the time, even as Jesus himself did not know it. When the Master comes, it may be early or late, but it will be night.' All the hours mentioned are hours in the night. 'This is applicable to us in particular at our death as well as to the general judgement. Our life is a night, a dark night, compared with the other life' (H). The Christians in Rome had also to be prepared for arrest or for a raid on their assembly and a call to martyrdom.

14 We come now to the narrative of the Passion of our Lord (Latin *passio*=suffering), culminating as it does in the Resurrection. It is the climax of the Gospel story. Whereas hitherto, as we have seen, Mark's gospel mainly consists of independent units or paragraphs (technically called *pericopae* from the Greek word for 'sections') which he has strung together according to his discretion, here we have a continuous story. It is generally agreed that the Passion narrative was the first part of the Gospel story to acquire a settled shape and order, as is shown by the fact that, broadly speaking, all four gospels are agreed about the course of events. There are clear reasons why this should have been so.

While eventually the fact that Christ had suffered and died and sacrificed his life was seen to be the chief wonder and glory of the Christian message, at first sight the crucifixion was a grave scandal and a bewildering mystery. Therefore the Christian preachers concentrated their attention upon it, and they found that the best way of meeting the questions that their hearers asked was to tell the whole story so as to show what actually happened, how innocent Jesus had been of the charges that had been

139

laid against him, and with what patience and courage
he had faced his sufferings. They were also at pains to
claim that the Passion had been in accordance with God's
will and with Old Testament prophecy.

At the same time the four evangelists tell the story, each
in his own style, with different emphases and interpretative
additions and modifications. Mark's version is the earliest
and he of course did not know (as we do) how the later
evangelists would handle the material. Characteristic of
Mark's version are the unadorned restraint and simplicity
with which he tells the story, the grim realism with which
he shows Jesus to have been increasingly isolated, rejected
and finally abandoned, deprived even of his Father's
presence, and his unemotional language. In Mark's gospel
no human sympathy is shown to Jesus; there is no divine
intervention on his behalf. Other evangelists found this so
intolerable that they sought to lighten the darkness, e.g.
by introducing an angel in Gethsemane, the women of
Jerusalem to sympathize with Jesus, and the penitent thief
(there is none of this in Mark), and by substituting for the
cry of dereliction on the cross words of confidence and
even of triumph. There is every reason to suppose that
Mark's version is nearest to the facts of the case.

14:1 It was now two days before the Passover and the
feast of Unleavened Bread. And the chief priests and the
scribes were seeking how to arrest him by stealth, and
kill him; 2 for they said, 'Not during the feast, lest there
be a tumult of the people.'

14:1 The Passover was the annual commemoration of
the deliverance of the people of Israel from bondage in
Egypt – their birth as a nation, their Independence Day. It
was observed on Nisan 15 which began at sundown on the
previous evening. It was combined with the springtime
agricultural festival of Unleavened Bread, which continued for a whole week – see Leviticus 23:5f. On the late
afternoon of Nisan 14 the lambs were slaughtered and

offered in the Temple, and the meal followed between sun-down and midnight. It had to be eaten in Jerusalem – see Deuteronomy 16:2f. *The chief priests and the scribes were seeking how to arrest him* This was on Wednesday. They designed to arrest Jesus privately to avoid *a tumult of the people* who were enthusiastic about Jesus and were now assembling for the festival. In Mark's first draft v. 10 may have followed v. 2, i.e. before he decided to insert the story of the anointing of Jesus here. It is differently placed in Luke and John.

3 And while he was at Bethany in the house of Simon the leper, as he sat at table, a woman came with an alabaster flask of ointment of pure nard, very costly, and she broke the flask and poured it over his head. 4 But there were some who said to themselves indignantly, 'Why was the ointment thus wasted? 5 For this ointment might have been sold for more than three hundred denarii, and given to the poor.' And they reproached her. 6. But Jesus said, 'Let her alone; why do you trouble her? She has done a beautiful thing to me. 7 For you always have the poor with you, and whenever you will, you can do good to them; but you will not always have me. 8 She has done what she could; she has anointed my body beforehand for burying. 9 And truly, I say to you, wherever the gospel is preached in the whole world, what she has done will be told in memory of her.'

14:3 *While he was at Bethany* Nothing else is known of Simon the leper. There are no good grounds for the con-jecture that he was Martha's husband, though this would go some way towards reconciling Mark's account with John 12:2.

An alabaster flask of ointment of pure nard Nard was an especially expensive perfume made from an Indian plant. The meaning of the Greek word translated 'pure' is uncertain: it might mean genuine, liquid, or distilled. Anointing parts of the body with unguents of one kind or another was and is a common practice in the East.

She broke the flask Presumably she knocked off the head of the flask: it would not be needed again. But Renan said that she did this in accordance with an old custom, which he had himself witnessed, viz. the breaking of vessels that had been used in the service of distinguished strangers. *And poured it over his head* Anointing the head was a sign of royal dignity (as at a coronation) and it is possible that the woman's action should be regarded as a symbolic recognition of the messiahship of Jesus. It has even been suggested that the woman was an enthusiastic follower of Jesus who meant to anoint him as king, having in mind the circumstances in which Jehu was anointed: see 2 Kings 9:6.

14:5 *This ointment might have been sold* A natural utilitarian reaction – with which most people, who are honest, will sympathize (?).

14:7 *You always have the poor with you* Cp. Deuteronomy 15:11. How far can this saying be held to justify church expenditure on ceremonial and ornaments?

14:8 *She has anointed my body beforehand for burying* Since there was no opportunity of anointing his body after his death, this anointing came to be regarded as rectifying the omission in advance. Some regard vv. 8f. as additions to the original form of the story. Stories of this kind usually ended with a single memorable pronouncement like that in vv. 6f. It also is questionable whether Jesus would have foreseen that his corpse would not be anointed in the normal way.

14:9 This too seems like an addition. Mark was thinking of the Church in his own time, when this episode was a regular part of the Passion story.

10 Then Judas Iscariot, who was one of the twelve, went to the chief priests in order to betray him to them. 11 And when they heard it they were glad, and promised to give him money. And he sought an opportunity to betray him.

What was it that Judas betrayed? It is generally sup-. posed that he told the Jewish authorities how they might arrest Jesus quietly, and this may be correct since amid the crowds of pilgrims in Jerusalem for the festival it would not be easy. On the other hand, it seems unlikely that the authorities would have to go to the length of bribing one of the disciples in order to achieve their purpose. Suggestions have therefore been made that Judas in fact betrayed something of much greater importance, namely that in private Jesus had claimed to be Messiah. In other words, Judas betrayed the messianic secret and so gave the High Priest confidence to ask the question in 14:61. There is also the question: Why did Judas betray Jesus? The usual answer, for which the New Testament provides support, is that he was motivated by avarice. So, for example, M. Henry wrote: 'Perhaps it was Judas's covetousness that brought him at first to follow Christ, having a promise that he should be cash-keeper or purser to the society, and he loved in his heart to be fingering money; and now there was money to be got on the other side, he was as ready to betray him as ever he had been to follow him.' But is it likely that Jesus would have chosen as one of his disciples a man who was capable of petty pilfering? So it has been suggested that it was disillusion that turned Judas into a traitor. Jesus was not turning out to be the kind of messiah that he had bargained for. However, the early Christians accepted cupidity as his motive.

12 And on the first day of Unleavened Bread, when they sacrificed the passover lamb, his disciples said to him, 'Where will you have us go and prepare for you to eat the passover?' 13 And he sent two of his disciples, and said to them, 'Go into the city, and a man carrying a jar of water will meet you; follow him, 14 and wherever he enters, say to the householder, "The Teacher says, where is my guest room, where I am to eat the passover with my disciples?" 15 And he will show you a large

upper room furnished and ready; there prepare for us.'
16 And the disciples set out and went into the city, and
found it as he had told them; and they prepared the
passover.

14:12 *On the first day of Unleavened Bread, when they
sacrificed the passover* According to Mark it is clear that
the Last Supper was a passover meal, and this might never
have been doubted, were it not that the fourth gospel says
equally clearly (see John 13:1; 18:28; 19:14) that it was
not the passover but a meal that Jesus had with his disciples on the preceding evening. Whether Mark or John
is right is a very complicated question, about which scholars
are still much divided. On the one hand, it is pointed out
that Mark makes no mention of the passover lamb in his
account of the Last Supper. On the other hand, it can be
said that John had an obvious motive for changing Mark's
chronology. He wanted Jesus to be crucified at the very
time when the passover lambs were being slain, on the
theological ground that he was the true passover lamb.
There are many other points of detail that are argued on
both sides of the question, which it would be tedious – and
also inconclusive – to specify here. Any one who wishes to
have them set out may be referred to Joachim Jeremias,
The Eucharistic Words of Jesus, chapter 1.

14:13 *A man carrying a jar of water will meet you*
Jars or pitchers of water were not usually carried by men,
but by women, so that this would be an exceptional sight.
Mark probably regarded it as an instance of Jesus's supernatural knowledge, but it could be the outcome of a previous arrangement. It was in accord with Jewish custom
that pilgrims could ask any householder in Jerusalem for
a room in which to eat the passover. 'No doubt the inhabitants of Jerusalem had rooms fitted up to be let out
for the occasion to those who came out of the country
to keep the passover, and one of those Christ made use
of . . . Probably he went where he was not known, that
he might be undisturbed with his disciples' (H).

14:15 *A large upper room furnished* with divans for reclining and strewn with carpets and cushions. Medieval and later paintings of the Last Supper, e.g. Leonardo da Vinci's, reflect contemporary furnishings and table arrangements.

17 And when it was evening he came with the twelve. 18 And as they were at table eating, Jesus said, 'Truly, I say to you, one of you will betray me, one who is eating with me.' 19 They began to be sorrowful, and to say to him one after another, 'Is it I?' 20 He said to them, 'It is one of the twelve, one who is dipping bread into the dish with me. 21 For the Son of man goes as it is written of him, but woe to the man by whom the Son of man is betrayed! It would have been better for that man if he had not been born.'

14:18 *One of you will betray me* Mark is concerned to show that Jesus was not taken by surprise by the treachery of Judas, and also that it was in accord with the divine will and had been predicted in the Old Testament (note *as it is written of him* in v. 21; see Psalm 41:9).

14:19 *Is it I?* 'Surely it is not I?' brings out the sense of the question better.

14:20 *One who is dipping bread into the dish with me* This refers to the custom by which guests reclining on couches or cushions used pieces of flat bread on which to get the contents of the dish which at the passover would be a sauce compounded of dates, raisins and vinegar. To betray a companion after eating with him was the grossest kind of perfidy.

14:21 *Woe to that man* Although Judas's treachery was part of a divinely ordained plan, that did not mean that he was not responsible for his action. This is an instance of the paradox of both divine predestination and human freedom being maintained together. The Pharisees had a saying, 'All is foreseen and free will is given', which holds together both sides of the paradox without resolving it. Is this the best that can be done?

22 And as they were eating, he took bread, and blessed, and broke it, and gave it to them, and said, 'Take; this is my body.' 23 And he took a cup, and when he had given thanks he gave it to them, and they all drank of it. 24 And he said to them, 'This is my blood of the covenant, which is poured out for many. 25 Truly, I say to you, I shall not drink again of the fruit of the vine until that day when I drink it new in the kingdom of God.'

14:22 The disciples are about to be deprived of the visible presence of Jesus: henceforth the broken bread and the wine outpoured are to be the pledge and means of effecting his real presence with them. *He took bread, and blessed* i.e. said grace over it. For the Jewish grace, see note on 6:41. *And he broke it, and gave it to them* He broke the loaf in pieces so that each participant could receive a piece. The early Church came to see profound symbolism in the breaking of the bread. It symbolized both the intimate relationship between the one Christ and his many members, and also the breaking of his body in the Passion. *This is my body* In Aramaic the verb was not expressed. Hence the disagreement about the precise meaning of the words cannot be settled by appeal to the Greek or English translations. 'On the whole, the least unsatisfactory translation is Moffatt's: "Take this, it means my body"' (T).

Between vv. 22 and 23 the passover meal will have been eaten. Mark's readers will not have been interested in that, since Christians did not continue the Jewish rites. They were interested in the institution of the eucharist which was the core and centre of their common worship and of their life together.

14:23 *When he had given thanks* This is a translation of a single Greek word *eucharistesas*, from which the word 'eucharist' is derived (cp. note on 8:6).

14:24 *This is my blood of the covenant* A.V. reads 'This is my blood of the new Testament'. The word 'new' is not in the best manuscripts, but it is a correct interpretation of what was meant. The Greek word translated 'testament' or 'covenant' meant 'will' or 'testament' in classical Greek, but it was used in the Greek Bible for the Hebrew word for 'covenant', which is how it should be translated. The idea of covenant plays an important part in the Bible, and the Methodists do well to remind themselves and other Christians of its importance with their annual covenant service. It speaks of the bond between God and his people: God binds himself to bless them and they are bound to serve him in gratitude. In the Old Testament the covenant was repeatedly renewed – with Noah, Moses, Joshua, and so on. The background to the idea of 'the new covenant', with which we are here concerned, is to be seen in Exodus 24:3-8, where God renewed his covenant with his people through the ministry of Moses and inaugurated it with sacrificial blood. The Messiah is the minister of the new covenant that had been promised in Jeremiah (31:31ff.), and he is now inaugurating it with his own sacrificial blood; see Hebrews 9:15-22. It should always be remembered that in the Bible (sacrificial) blood stands not so much for the death as for the dedicated life of the victim (cp. Leviticus 17:14). *Which is poured out for many* Neither Hebrew nor Aramaic has a word for 'all' in the plural. 'Many is here equivalent to 'all'; cp. note on 10:45.

14:25 *Until that day when I drink it new in the kingdom of God* Everything in the kingdom of God will be new. Jesus looked forward beyond his death to the consummation of all things in the kingdom, which, as we have seen, could be pictured as the messianic banquet, an allusion to which may be implied in these words.

26 And when they had sung a hymn, they went out to the Mount of Olives. 27 And Jesus said to them, 'You

will all fall away; for it is written, "I will strike the shepherd, and the sheep will be scattered." 28 But after I am raised up, I will go before you to Galilee.' 29 Peter said to him, 'Even though they all fall away, I will not.' 30 And Jesus said to him, 'Truly, I say to you, this very night, before the cock crows twice, you will deny me three times.' 31 But he said vehemently, 'If I must die with you, I will not deny you.' And they all said the same.

14:26 *When they had sung a hymn* i.e. part of the Hallel psalms (114-118) which were sung at the end of the passover meal. Barclay translates: 'when they had sung the psalm of praise.' 'This was Christ's swan-like song, which he sang just before he entered upon his agony' (H).

14:27 *Jesus said to them, 'You will all fall away'* We are so familiar with the fact that the disciples failed and deserted Jesus in the final crisis that we forget what a difficulty this must have been for the early Christians, who had good reason to venerate the Lord's apostles. The idea that it was all part of the divine plan, as had been prophesied in scripture, brought them relief. The reference here is to Zechariah 13:7 (slightly modified, perhaps when it was included in a collection of Christian proof-texts).

14:28 *After I am raised up, I will go before you to Galilee* This verse has given rise to much discussion. It breaks the connection between vv. 27 and 29. Some think it was inserted here to prepare the way for 16:7, by an early editor who wanted to insist that the resurrection appearances took place in Galilee, not in Jerusalem as Luke's gospel says. This view is supported by the consideration that in v. 29 Peter entirely disregards v. 28. *I will go before you to Galilee* has several possible meanings. (i) 'I shall go before you into Galilee and shall appear to you there'. (ii) 'I will place myself at your head and lead you to Galilee', i.e. an unfulfilled prediction. (iii) In view of the fact that Galilee was associated with the Gentiles (see Isaiah 9:1; Matthew 4:15), it might mean that the risen Christ would lead his followers in a world-wide mission. (iv) Some scholars think that Galilee was held to be the likely scene of the *Parousia*, and that the meaning here is that the disciples were to wait there in anticipation of what was believed to be this imminent event.

14:29 Peter is responding to Jesus's statement that they would all fall away.

14:30 *Before the cock crows twice* There is evidence that the keeping of cocks was prohibited in Jerusalem at this time; so cock-crow may have been used as a conventional mark of time (see 13:35), although Mark apparently took it literally. The bugle call for the changing of the guard in the fortress of Antonia was also known as 'cock-crowing'. If a cock actually crowed twice, why did not Peter remember at the first?

32 And they went to a place which was called Gethsemane; and he said to his disciples, 'Sit here, while I pray.' 33 And he took with him Peter and James and John, and began to be greatly distressed and troubled. 34 And he said to them, 'My soul is very sorrowful, even to death; remain here, and watch.' 35 And going a little farther, he fell on the ground and prayed that, if it were possible, the hour might pass from him. 36 And he said, 'Abba, Father, all things are possible to thee; remove this cup from me; yet not what I will, but what thou wilt.' 37 And he came and found them sleeping, and he said to Peter, 'Simon, are you asleep? Could you not watch one hour? 38 Watch and pray that you may not enter into temptation; the spirit indeed is willing, but the flesh is weak.' 39 And again he went away and prayed, saying the same words. 40 And again he came and found them sleeping, for their eyes were very heavy; and they did not know what to answer him. 41 And he came the third time, and said to them, 'Are you still sleeping

and taking your rest? It is enough; the hour has come;
the Son of man is betrayed into the hands of sinners.
42 Rise, let us be going; see, my betrayer is at hand.'

14:32 *Gethsemane* means an oil press, probably an olive
grove. *He said to his disciples* i.e. to the remaining eight.

14:33 *He took with him Peter and James and John*
'These three had bragged most of their ability and willing-
ness to suffer with him' (H). *And he began to be greatly
distressed* The word denotes 'being in the grip of shudder-
ing horror in the face of the dreadful prospect before him'
(Cr).

14:34 *My soul is very sorrowful, even to death* so that
death seemed preferable; cp. Jonah 4:9. *And watch* i.e.
keep awake.

14:35 *And going a little farther* 'The intensity of the
anguish drives him from them to seek peace before the
face of his Father' (T). *The hour* It was the hour of
destiny, doomsday, the hour of apparent calamity which
was to be the hour of salvation.

14:36 *And he said, 'Abba, Father'* 'Abba' was a homely
Aramaic word, which would have been regarded as dis-
respectful if addressed to God. Phillips and Barclay translate: 'Dear Father'. *'Abba, Father'*, i.e. with the translation of the Aramaic, was for the benefit of Greek-speaking
Christians. There are other echoes of the Lord's Prayer
in Gethsemane in addition to this: 'thy will be done'; 'lead
us not into temptation'. As regards the question of how
the disciples could have known the words of Jesus's
prayer, it has been said that 'if they were not physically
close enough to Jesus to hear the words of his prayer, then,
later, they must have been spiritually close enough to
interpret the scene aright.'

14:37 *He said to Peter, 'Simon, are you asleep?'* He
has not been called 'Simon' since 3:16, but at this point
he is Peter (rock-man) no more. He who was ready to die
with Jesus had not the strength to keep awake with him
for one hour.

14:38 *Into temptation* i.e. the time of severe trial that was expected to precede the *Parousia* (cp. 13:14-20; Revelation 3:10). *The spirit indeed is willing, but the flesh is weak* The suggestion that the words were spoken by Jesus of himself is interesting but improbable. In that case the first half of the verse may originally have read: 'Pray that I may not enter into temptation (or the time of trial)'. More probably the words apply to the disciples, but it is not clear whether 'the spirit' means the Spirit of God or the human spirit, i.e. the higher part of man's nature contrasted with the lower (the flesh). 'For the Church of Mark's day the example of Jesus in the Garden, as contrasted with the behaviour of the three disciples, must have had special value as setting forth the spirit in which the vocation to martyrdom should be approached' (R).

14:39 *And again he went away* 'Jesus is alone on earth, without any to feel or share his pain, without any even to know it; heaven and he are alone in that knowledge' (Pascal).

14:40 *For their eyes were very heavy* – as a consequence of the hearty passover meal?

14:41 *Are you still sleeping and taking your rest? It is enough* 'Still asleep? still resting? No more of that!' (M). The meaning of the word translated 'it is enough' or 'no more of that!' is uncertain. Other possible translations are: 'It is all over' (J) and 'He has had his pay' (Ba: referring to Judas). *The hour has come* – see note on v. 35.

14:42 *Rise, let us be going* 'Get up! Let us go!' (J), i.e. to meet them.

43 And immediately, while he was still speaking, Judas came, one of the twelve, and with him a crowd with swords and clubs, from the chief priests and the scribes and the elders. 44 Now the betrayer had given them a sign, saying, 'The one I shall kiss is the man; seize him and lead him away under guard.' 45 And when he came, he went up to him at once, and said, 'Master!'

And he kissed him. 46 And they laid hands on him and seized him. 47 But one of those who stood by drew his sword, and struck the slave of the high priest and cut off his ear. 48 And Jesus said to them, 'Have you come out as against a robber, with swords and clubs to capture me? 49 Day after day I was with you in the temple teaching, and you did not seize me. But let the scriptures be fulfilled.' 50 And they all forsook him, and fled.

14:43 *With him a crowd with swords and clubs* It sounds like a rather motley rabble, but they do not seem to have been disorderly.

14:44 *The one I shall kiss is the man* This was how a rabbi was greeted by his disciples. Jesus could not otherwise have been readily identifiable in the dark. It may be implied that Judas held Jesus long enough to enable everyone present to see him. 'Judas betrayed him with a kiss; abusing the freedom Christ used to allow his disciples of kissing his cheek at their return, when they had any time been absent' (H). *Lead him away under guard* See that he does not escape.

14:47 *But one of those who stood by drew his sword* Evidently one of those present who was well disposed to Jesus. It is implied that there was some sort of scuffle or skirmish. The later evangelists named both the assailant and the assailed and otherwise built up the incident, providing it with a miraculous conclusion. It is a good example of how a story can quickly be embellished in the course of transmission.

14:48 *Have you come out as against a robber?* 'Do you take me for a bandit?' (N.E.B.) is a better translation.

14:49 *Day after day I was with you in the temple* But according to Mark Jesus has been in the Temple on only three days. He must have been in Jerusalem longer than Mark's account allows: cp. note on 11:8. *Let the scriptures be fulfilled* The reference may be to Isaiah 53, but may be quite general since by the time Mark wrote the idea was firmly established that the Passion was a fulfilment of prophecy: e.g. see I Corinthians 15:3.

14:50 *They all forsook him, and fled* Mark brings out more insistently than the other gospels that Jesus was increasingly isolated and alone, bereft of every human support.

> 51 And a young man followed him, with nothing but a linen cloth about his body; and they seized him, but he left the linen cloth and ran away naked.

This is a mysterious incident which cannot be satisfactorily explained. It used to be conjectured that Mark himself was the young man in question, and this is like the artist's signature in the corner of his painting: an attractive but unwarranted speculation. Another suggestion has been that it was John, the beloved disciple. About that Calvin wrote severely: 'How some persons have come to dream that this was John I know not, nor is it of much importance to enquire. The chief point is, to ascertain for what purpose Mark has related this transaction. I think that his object was, to inform us that those wicked men – as usually happens in riotous assemblies – stormed and raved without shame or modesty; which appeared from their seizing a young man who was unknown to them, and not suspected of any crime.' This may be right, or we may agree with Branscomb that 'one can only guess that the young man was one of the witnesses and narrators of the story of the arrest, and his experience was both known and remembered'. The notion that the incident was invented as a fulfilment of Amos 2:16 seems very farfetched.

14:53-65 Many involved questions surround the trial and condemnation of Jesus. For one thing the gospels themselves vary in what they say. This is not surprising. Neither the evangelists nor their informants had been able to be present and witness the proceedings, still less to be behind the scenes, and what went on behind the scenes may have been of most consequence. The only thing that was certain was that Jesus had been crucified. Then, while Mark clearly gives the impression that there was a formal trial before the Sanhedrin, what he tells us does not conform to what we know of Jewish law concerning a judicial trial (fourteen unlikely points of detail have been noted). It is also uncertain whether or not at this time the Sanhedrin could inflict capital punishment. If it could, there is the question why then they handed Jesus over to the Roman authorities. There is also a marked tendency in the gospels and in Acts to make the Jewish, rather than the Roman, authorities responsible for the death of Jesus. This may have led to an exaggerated account of the Sanhedrin's proceedings. There was an obvious desire in the early Church to assure the Roman authorities that they had nothing to fear from Christian missionary activity.

It seems probable that Jesus was examined informally or privately in the High Priest's house by those members of the Sanhedrin who could be present on passover night, and that the decision was then taken to denounce Jesus before Pilate as the most expeditious way of doing away with him. Or perhaps this informal meeting of members of the Sanhedrin was not held until the morning.

53 And they led Jesus to the high priest; and all the chief priests and the elders and the scribes were assembled. 54 And Peter had followed him at a distance, right into the courtyard of the high priest; and he was sitting with the guards, and warming himself at the fire. 55 Now the chief priests and the whole council sought testimony against Jesus to put him to death; but they found none. 56 For many bore false witness against him, and their witness did not agree. 57 And some stood up and bore false witness against him, saying, 58 'We heard him say, "I will destroy this temple that is made with hands, and in three days I will build another, not made with hands." ' 59 Yet not even so did their testimony agree. 60 And the high priest stood up in the

midst, and asked Jesus, 'Have you no answer to make? What is it that these men testify against you?' 61 But he was silent and made no answer. Again the high priest asked him, 'Are you the Christ, the Son of the Blessed?' 62 And Jesus said, 'I am; and you will see the Son of man seated at the right hand of Power, and coming with the clouds of heaven.' 63 And the high priest tore his garments, and said, 'Why do we still need witnesses? 64 You have heard his blasphemy. What is your decision?' And they all condemned him as deserving death. 65 And some began to spit on him, and to cover his face, and to strike him, saying to him, 'Prophesy!' And the guards received him with blows.

14:53 *They led Jesus to the high priest* Mark nowhere gives his name. *And all the chief priests and the elders and the scribes were assembled* This implies a formal meeting of the whole Sanhedrin. There were seventy-one members, who could hardly be got together on passover night, and anyhow it was illegal to hold a session during a festival or at night.

14:54 *Peter had followed him . . . right into the courtyard* The house or palace will have been built round an open courtyard. *He was sitting with the guards, and warming himself at the fire* 'There he sat in the firelight with the servants, keeping himself warm' (P). The light of the fire lit up his features.

14:55 *The whole council sought testimony against Jesus* One would have expected the evidence to have been collected and prepared beforehand, not to be looked for at the last moment and at dead of night.

14:56 *Their witness did not agree* By Jewish law the agreement of two witnesses was required; see Deuteronomy 17:6. Has the narrative been influenced by Psalm 27:12?

14:58 *We heard him say, 'I will destroy this temple . . .'* Cp. 13:2. Just what Jesus had said is not certain, but, although Mark says it was a matter of 'false witness', a saying of Jesus to this effect was well known in the early Church. Stephen also was charged with a similar saying: Acts 6:13f.

14:61 *But he was silent and made no answer* Jesus may have been aware of the futility of defence. Cp. Psalm 38:12ff.

14:62 *And Jesus said, 'I am'* The messianic secret is a secret no longer. The Jewish authorities are represented as having either suspected or known that Jesus made messianic claims. Perhaps this is what Judas had betrayed; see note on 14:10. *You will see the Son of man* See Daniel 7:13.

14:63 *The high priest tore his garments* 'Originally a sign of passionate grief, this gesture became a formal judicial act in the case of the High Priest and is closely regulated in the later law books' (N).

14:64 *You have heard his blasphemy* But to claim to be Messiah was not blasphemy in the technical sense; this may explain why the Jewish authorities could not proceed with this charge, and decided to denounce Jesus to Pilate on another one. 'They could only *show their teeth*, they could not *bite*' (H).

14:65 *Some began to spit on him* Presumably some of the slaves who held Jesus bound. *Saying to him, 'Prophesy!'* i.e. play the prophet now. *The guards received him with blows* This probably means that the servants took him into custody with blows.

66 And as Peter was below in the courtyard, one of the maids of the high priest came; 67 and seeing Peter warming himself, she looked at him, and said, 'You also were with the Nazarene, Jesus.' 68 But he denied it, saying, 'I neither know nor understand what you mean.' And he went out into the gateway. 69 And the maid saw him, and began again to say to the bystanders, 'This man is one of them.' 70 But again he denied it. And after a little while again the bystanders said to Peter, 'Certainly you are one of them; for you are a Galilean.'

71 But he began to invoke a curse on himself and to swear, 'I do not know this man of whom you speak.' 72 And immediately the cock crowed a second time. And Peter remembered how Jesus had said to him, 'Before the cock crows twice, you will deny me three times.' And he broke down and wept.

14:66 *As Peter was below in the courtyard* i.e. of the High Priest's palace. Peter's fall, said Calvin, 'is a bright mirror of our weakness'.

14:68 *I neither know nor understand what you mean* i.e. what you are talking about. Peter does not yet deny his knowledge of Jesus, as he will in v. 71.

14:69 *The maid saw him, and began again to say to the bystanders* Her suspicions have been aroused and she pursues the matter.

14:70 *You are a Galilean* Galilean Aramaic differed from Judean as northern English does from southern.

14:71 *He began to invoke a curse on himself and to swear On himself* is not in the Greek. The meaning may be that he called down a curse on himself if he was not telling the truth and/or on those who alleged that he was a follower of Jesus.

14:72 *The cock crowed a second time* – see note on 14:30. *He broke down* This is the most likely meaning of a curious expression. Other possible translations are 'rushing outside'; 'casting himself on the ground'; 'casting all restraint away'; 'he burst into tears'. 'When he thought thereon' (A.V. and R.V.) is very weak.

15:1 And as soon as it was morning the chief priests, with the elders and scribes, and the whole council held a consultation; and they bound Jesus and led him away and delivered him to Pilate. 2 And Pilate asked him, 'Are you the King of the Jews?' And he answered him, 'You have said so.' 3 And the chief priests accused him of many things. 4 And Pilate again asked him, 'Have you no answer to make? See how many charges they bring against you.' 5 But Jesus made no further answer, so that Pilate wondered.

15:1 *As soon as it was morning* 'The unwearied industry of wicked men in doing that which is evil should shame us for our backwardness and slothfulness in that which is good. They that war against Christ and thy soul are up early: how long wilt thou sleep, o sluggard?' (H). *The whole council held a consultation* This is more likely to have been an informal gathering of those members who were available (see note above). *Delivered him to Pilate* Roman law courts began their proceedings at dawn. Mark takes it for granted that his readers would know that Pilate was the procurator. Although Jewish writers described Pilate as 'avaricious, cruel and inflexible', and he was recalled in A.D. 36 on charges of maladministration, the evangelists do not represent him in an unfavourable light, and the Abyssinian church canonized him as a saint! He may be regarded as an average representative of civil government. The procurator normally resided at Caesarea, but came to Jerusalem at passover time to ensure order.

15:2 *Are you the King of the Jews?* The *you* is emphatic, and perhaps ironical. Mark does not actually say what charge or charges the Jewish authorities laid against Jesus, but it is implied that they said he claimed to be 'King of the Jews', which was to give his claim to messiahship a strictly political character that Pilate would have to take seriously. *And he answered him, 'You have said so'* While there has been much debate about the meaning of this reply, there can be little doubt that it was intended to be non-committal. Jesus could not say 'Yes', for that would be taken to mean that he claimed to be a political messiah; he could not say 'No', for that would be taken as a denial of messiahship altogether.

15:5 *But Jesus made no further answer* Christians have always seen in this a fulfilment of Isaiah 53:7. 'Christ was silent, in order that he might open our mouths by his silence: for hence arises that distinguished privilege of which Paul speaks in such magnificent terms that we can boldly cry Abba Father' (Ca).

6 Now at the feast he used to release for them one prisoner for whom they asked. 7 And among the rebels in prison, who had committed murder in the insurrection, there was a man called Barabbas. 8 And the crowd came up and began to ask Pilate to do as he was wont to do for them. 9 And he answered them, 'Do you want me to release for you the King of the Jews?' 10 For he perceived that it was out of envy that the chief priests had delivered him up. 11 But the chief priests stirred up the crowd to have him release for them Barabbas instead. 12 And Pilate again said to them, 'Then what shall I do with the man whom you call the King of the Jews?' 13 And they cried out again, 'Crucify him.' 14 And Pilate said to them, 'Why, what evil has he done?' But they shouted all the more, 'Crucify him.' 15 So Pilate, wishing to satisfy the crowd, released for them Barabbas; and having scourged Jesus, he delivered him to be crucified.

15:6 *At the feast he used to release for them one prisoner* Nothing else is known of this supposed custom. Perhaps the evangelists inferred from this incident that it was a regular practice. There is an interesting suggestion that what actually happened was that a group of Barabbas's supporters arrived on the scene at this moment to ask for his release. (Make sure that you pronounce his name Bar-Abbas, not Barrabbas, as is commonly done.) There is some evidence that his real name was 'Jesus Barabbas', and it could originally have stood in the Passion narrative. Jesus (Joshua) was quite a common name, but by the time Mark wrote the name of Jesus was regarded as so sacred that its use by Barabbas would have been looked upon as offensive and could easily have been suppressed. When the supporters of Barabbas on this occasion called for the release of 'Jesus', meaning Barabbas, Pilate may at first

have thought that they were asking for the release of the
Jesus who was before him, hence his question in v. 9:
Do you want me to release for you the King of the Jews?
The suggestion is that the priests then did a deal with the
leaders of Barabbas's supporters, undertaking to join with
them in their appeal for his release, if they would join in
demanding the crucifixion of Jesus. While this reconstruc-
tion of the course of events is conjectural, it makes good
sense of vv. 6-15.

15:14 *Pilate said to them, 'Why, what evil has he done?'*
Note that the Roman authority testifies to the innocence
of Jesus. 'The fact of the execution of their leader and
founder by the Roman Government was an embarrassment
to the Christian cause which it was one of the functions of
the Passion narrative to mitigate as much as possible'
(Br).

15:15 *So Pilate, wishing to satisfy the crowd* Mark
gives us to understand that it was the pressure of the mob
that made Pilate weakly give way to the demand of the
priests. *Having scourged Jesus* Scourging was the normal
prelude to crucifixion. 'This cruel punishment was in-
flicted with whips of leather loaded with stone or metal,
while the victim was sometimes bound to a pillar' (T).

16 And the soldiers led him away inside the palace
(that is, the praetorium); and they called together the
whole battalion. 17 And they clothed him in a purple
cloak, and plaiting a crown of thorns they put it on
him. 18 And they began to salute him, 'Hail, King of
the Jews!' 19 And they struck his head with a reed, and
spat upon him, and they knelt down in homage to him.
20 And when they had mocked him, they stripped him
of the purple cloak, and put his own clothes on him. And
they led him out to crucify him.

15:16 *The praetorium* A Latin word for the governor's
residence. It is implied that hitherto the proceedings had
taken place in the open air. *The whole battalion* A word

used for a cohort, a body of troops several hundreds strong, but here probably used loosely.

15:17 *A purple cloak* Kings wear purple or scarlet, so a soldier's scarlet military cloak did duty for the purple of royalty. *A crown of thorns* Kings wear crowns, so they made a crown perhaps out of firewood, mimicking the laurel wreath worn by the emperor.

15:18 *Hail, King of the Jews!* Kings are attended by the acclamations of their subjects. '*Ave, rex judaeorum*' was a parody of '*Ave, Caesar imperator*'.

15:19 *They struck his head with a reed* Kings carry a sceptre, so they smote his head with a reed. *And spat upon him* Subjects when they swear allegiance kiss their sovereigns, so they spat upon him in derision: cp. Isaiah 50:6. *And they knelt down in homage* Kings are wont to be addressed upon the knee.

15:20 *They led him out to crucify him* 'What is the mystery which lies hid under the fact, that our gracious Saviour was led out of the city, no mortal man . . . would have been likely to have discovered, had not the wisdom of the apostle instructed us on the subject, Hebrews 13:11-14' (Be). 'Jesus Christ was not merely murdered by hooligans in a country road; he was condemned by everything that was most respectable in that day, everything that pretended to be most righteous – the religious leaders of the time, the authority of the Roman government, and even the democracy itself which shouted to save Barabbas rather than Christ' (Herbert Butterfield).

21 And they compelled a passer-by, Simon of Cyrene, who was coming in from the country, the father of Alexander and Rufus, to carry his cross. 22 And they brought him to the place called Golgotha (which means the place of a skull). 23 And they offered him wine mingled with myrrh; but he did not take it. 24 And they crucified him, and divided his garments among them, casting lots for them, to decide what each should take. 25 And it was the third hour, when they crucified

him. 26 And the inscription of the charge against him read, 'The King of the Jews.' 27 And with him they crucified two robbers, one on his right and one on his left. 29 And those who passed by derided him, wagging their heads, and saying, 'Aha! You who would destroy the temple and build it in three days, 30 save yourself, and come down from the cross!' 31 So also the chief priests mocked him to one another with the scribes, saying, 'He saved others, he cannot save himself. 32 Let the Christ, the King of Israel, come down now from the cross, that we may see and believe.' Those who were crucified with him also reviled him.

15:21 *They compelled a passer-by* They 'impressed' him: the word is a technical one. Those condemned to be crucified had to carry the cross-beam to the place of execution. It is implied that Jesus, as a result of the scourging and what he had already gone through, was unable to carry it himself. *Simon of Cyrene* was probably a pilgrim from Cyrene in north Africa, where there was a big Jewish colony. He was entering Jerusalem from his lodging in the country. One reason for his being mentioned may be that it showed the Christians had a reliable source of information about these events. *The father of Alexander and Rufus* They must have been known to the church for which Mark was writing. A Rufus is mentioned in Romans 16:13, but it was quite a common name.

15:22 *Golgotha* (. . . *the place of a skull*) It may have been so called from its shape. Jerome refers to a tradition according to which the skull of Adam was buried there, and in pictures of the crucifixion a skull is sometimes depicted at the foot of the cross. Jerome remarked that it was 'an attractive explanation (of the name), and one calculated to tickle the ears of the people, but not however true'. The Fathers were not as credulous as some suppose. As a piece of symbolism the idea was well conceived: 'As in Adam all die, so in Christ shall all be made alive.' M. Henry writing in the seventeenth century noted: 'It was the common place of execution, as Tyburn; for he was in all respects numbered with the transgressors.'

15:23 *They offered him wine mingled with myrrh* This was an old Jewish custom (see Proverbs 31:6f.), the purpose of which was to deaden pain, though there is some doubt whether the mixture indicated would have that effect. Jesus willed to die with unclouded mind.

15:24 *They crucified him* 'After being stripped of all his clothes (which became the property of the executioners), the victim was laid on the ground while his outstretched arms were fixed to the cross-beams by either nails or thongs. Next the cross-beam was lifted up with the body on it . . . Small wonder that Cicero described this as "the most cruel and frightful of punishments" ' (N). 'It is the greatness and heart of the Christian message that God, as manifest in the Christ on the Cross, totally participates in the dying of a child, in the condemnation of a criminal, in the disintegration of a mind, in starvation and famine, and even in the human rejection of himself' (P. Tillich). 'The cross has become so outwardly honoured since those days; such an object of worship and adoration; so rayed round with secular glory from the labours of poet and painter that St Paul's words, "God forbid that I should glory, save in the cross of our Lord Jesus Christ", do not sound so mad in our ears as they did in the ears of those who looked on crucifixion as we do on hanging or penal servitude, or who felt as little reverence for the cross as we do for the gallows or the tread-mill' (G. Tyrrell). *And divided his garments among them* See Psalm 22:18. It was the duty of the soldiers to stay on guard till death ensued, so as to prevent a rescue. They may have brought dice with them to while away the time and could have used them for *casting lots.*

15:25 *It was the third hour* i.e. 9 a.m.

15:26 *The inscription of the charge against him* It was the Roman practice that a tablet should be prepared, stating the grounds of a criminal's condemnation. It was carried in front of him on the way to execution and then displayed on the cross. *The King of the Jews* Calvin and others have remarked that Pilate was in this unwittingly a true preacher, as Caiaphas was a prophet (see John 11:51).

15:27 *With him they crucified two robbers* Verse 28, which quotes Isaiah 53:12, is missing from the best manuscripts, but Mark is likely to have had the quotation in mind.

15:29-32 These mocking taunts were also seen as a fulfilment of prophecy; see Lamentations 2:15; Wisdom 2:17f.; Psalm 22:7f. *The chief priests mocked him to one another with the scribes* 'These chief priests, one would think, might now have found themselves other work to do. If they would not go to do their duty in the temple, yet they might have been employed in an office not foreign to their profession; though they would not offer any counsel or comfort to the Lord Jesus, yet they might have given some help to the thieves in their dying moments . . . but they did not think that their business' (H). *Let the Christ . . . come down now from the cross* 'They would have believed in him, had he come down', said General Booth. 'We believe in him, because he stayed up.'

33 And when the sixth hour had come, there was darkness over the whole land until the ninth hour. 34 And at the ninth hour Jesus cried with a loud voice, 'Eloi, Eloi, lama sabachthani?' which means, 'My God, my God, why hast thou forsaken me?' 35 And some of the bystanders hearing it said, 'Behold, he is calling Elijah.' 36 And one ran and, filling a sponge full of vinegar, put it on a reed and gave it to him to drink, saying, 'Wait, let us see whether Elijah will come to take him down.' 37 And Jesus uttered a loud cry, and breathed his last. 38 And the curtain of the temple was torn in two, from top to bottom. 39 And when the centurion, who stood facing him, saw that he thus breathed his last, he said, 'Truly this man was the Son of God.' 40 There were also

women looking on from afar, among whom were Mary Magdalene, and Mary the mother of James the younger and of Joses, and Salome, 41 who, when he was in Galilee, followed him, and ministered to him; and also many other women who came up with him to Jerusalem.

15:33 *When the sixth hour had come* i.e. about noon. *There was darkness over the whole land* It is a mistake to look for a natural cause of this darkness. There could not be an eclipse at the time of the passover full moon. It is a poetic or symbolic darkness, showing the judgement of heaven on what was taking place; cp. Amos 8:9. 'There those glorious eyes grew faint in their light; so as the sun, ashamed to survive them, departed with his light too' (John Donne). 'When our Lord died, all creation, which held its life from him, necessarily felt the pangs of death also' (Coventry Patmore).

> The sunne holds down his head for shame,
> Dead with eclipses, when we speak of thee.
> (G. Herbert)

15:34 *My God, my God, why hast thou forsaken me?* Much has been written about the cry of dereliction. Albert Schweitzer supposed that Jesus was expecting God to intervene and bring in his final kingdom before his death; when this did not happen, he died of a broken heart. Another theory is that the original Passion story said that Jesus 'uttered a loud cry' (see v. 37) before his death, and that this was variously interpreted in the words from the cross reported in the different gospels. In Mark the Lord's cry is the first verse of Psalm 22, and some have thought it implies that on the cross Jesus recited the whole of that psalm, which would make the cry an expression of faith rather than of dereliction. Theologians have explained that Jesus underwent the experience of exclusion from God's presence or of separation from his Father, and that this was the result of his taking upon himself the sins of the whole world. Thus Cranfield comments: 'The burden of the world's sin, his complete self-identification with sinners, involved not merely a felt, but a real, abandonment by his Father. It is in the cry of dereliction that the full horror of man's sin stands revealed.' We may be sure that Mark did not regard it as a cry of ultimate despair. Rawlinson's conclusion is safest: 'On the assumption that our Lord really uttered the words it is better to say frankly that we do not know exactly what was in his mind at the time, that we are here face to face with the supreme mystery of the Saviour's Passion.'

15:35 *Behold, he is calling Elijah* It is true that in later legends Elijah was regarded as a helper in time of need. But would Roman soldiers have thought of Elijah? It has been conjectured that they may have thought that Jesus was calling on Helios, the Sun-God.

15:36 *Filling a sponge full of vinegar* Probably the drink that was provided for the refreshment of the soldiers during their long wait. But see Psalm 69:21b.

15:37 *Jesus uttered a loud cry* – the shout of a victor? *– and breathed his last* But Mark is describing a sudden violent death. N.E.B.'s 'and died' is much to be preferred and accords with the stark realism of Mark's account. 'He intended, by this loud and piercing exclamation, to assure us that his soul would be safe and uninjured in death, in order that we, supported by the same confidence, may cheerfully depart from the frail hovel of our flesh' (C).

Now that the Passion of Jesus, which Mark has related with grim and unrelieved realism, is complete, in two pregnant verses, the point of which a surface reader will miss, he proclaims its meaning and what is to be its outcome. Both the Jewish Temple and the gentile world, in the person of the Roman centurion, bear testimony to the messiahship of Jesus.

15:38 *The curtain of the temple was torn in two, from top to bottom* i.e. by no human hand. This is not to be understood materially any more than the darkness that was over all the land. The curtain or veil that hung in front of the Holy of Holies see Exodus 26 : 31-35), which was the shrine of the divine presence, and which was entered only once a year by the High Priest on the day of atonement, is now torn in two. The sacrificial death of the Messiah, who is the high priest of the whole world, has secured open access to the one God and Father of all – for all peoples and at all times. He has made the final atonement once and for all. See Hebrews 10 : 19-23.

The tearing of the curtain has also been seen as a sign of the impending destruction of the Temple, 'a presage to the unbelieving Jews of the utter destruction of their church and nation' (H).

15 : 39 *The centurion . . . said, 'Truly this man was the Son of God'* The earlier R.S.V. rendering was misleading (. . . *a son of God*); cp. 'This man was surely God's Son' (Wi). It is true that there is no definite article in the Greek, but this is in accord with Greek usage (see Cr). Mark intended this to be a declaration by a representative of the gentile world of the divine Sonship of Jesus. The centurion is the prototype and forerunner of countless multitudes who will be converted by the message of the cross. These two verses confirm what Mark had pointed forward to in his announcement in 1 : 1.

15 : 40 *There were also women looking on from afar* These women, who have not previously been mentioned by Mark, are introduced now not only to prepare the way for what is to follow, but to indicate that the Christians had reliable information about the crucifixion, albeit obtained from observers at a distance. *Mary Magdalene* The other evangelists will supply more information about her. *Mary the mother of James the younger and of Joses* This James (designated the younger to distinguish him from another James, perhaps the son of Zebedee) and Joses were presumably known to Mark's readers like Alexander and Rufus (see note on v. 21). *Salome* Mark does not identify

her further; Matthew (27:56) says that she was the mother of the sons of Zebedee.

42 And when evening had come, since it was the day of Preparation, that is, the day before the sabbath, 43 Joseph of Arimathea, a respected member of the council, who was also himself looking for the kingdom of God, took courage and went to Pilate, and asked for the body of Jesus. 44 And Pilate wondered if he were already dead; and summoning the centurion, he asked him whether he was already dead. 45 And when he learned from the centurion that he was dead, he granted the body to Joseph. 46 And he bought a linen shroud, and taking him down, wrapped him in the linen shroud, and laid him in a tomb which had been hewn out of the rock; and he rolled a stone against the door of the tomb. 47 Mary Magdalene and Mary the mother of Joses saw where he was laid.

15:42 *When evening had come* The indications of time are rather obscure. Mark probably meant about 4 p.m. on the Friday.

15:43 *Joseph of Arimathea* Nothing is known about him apart from this incident, nor about the location of Arimathea or whether it was his place of origin or residence. It was the Jewish practice always to bury the dead on the day of death, if possible. The bodies of those who were crucified might be handed over to friends or relatives, if they sought permission to remove them. Josephus tell us that 'the Jews are so careful about funeral rites that even criminals who have been sentenced to crucifixion are taken down and buried before sunset.' See Deuteronomy 21: 22f.

15:44 *Pilate wondered if he were already dead* Those who were crucified could often linger on for some days.

15:45 *He granted the body to Joseph* The Greek says not 'body' but 'corpse': Mark meant to insist on the stark reality of Jesus's death.

15:46 *He rolled a stone against the door of the tomb*
as a protection against wild beasts or thieves.

16 Here we must consider what has been described as
'the greatest of all literary mysteries'. Everyone who has
gone into the matter agrees that the authentic text of the
gospel ends at 16:8. What is printed after that in A.V. and
R.V. is a passage that was added in the second century by
someone who felt he must round off the gospel with an
account of the appearances of the Risen Lord. Beyond that
there is no agreement. On the one hand, there are those
who say that 'there can be no doubt that Mark recorded,
or intended to record, as the climax and conclusion of
the story the appearances of Jesus to the disciples in
their native district' (Br). Other commentators have used
equally strong and equally unwarranted language. It is
'inconceivable' says one, it is 'impossible' says another,
it is 'incredible' says a third, that the gospel was intended to end at 16:8. Their reason for saying this is
not only that they hold Mark must have recorded appearances of the Risen Lord; they also say that no author
would end his book so abruptly, moreover on a note of
fear and trembling (*for they were afraid*). The ending is
even more astonishing in Greek than in English, for in
Greek the last word is a conjunction which one is never
supposed to use at the end of a sentence, let alone of a
paragraph or a book. It is therefore conjectured that
Mark may have been arrested, or may have had a heart
attack, in the middle of a sentence and was unable to
finish his work and that no one finished it for him.
Alternatively, it is suggested that somehow or other the
last page of the book was lost, before any copies had
been made and before it came into the hands of Matthew
or Luke. Are these considerations conclusive? By no
means.

To take first the point about the way the last sentence
ends in Greek. It is true that this is extremely unusual,
but instances have been found in Greek literature which

show that from a linguistic point of view it cannot be pronounced an impossible ending. Anyhow, a writer who was attempting to convey th. ineffable truth about the Resurrection would be justified in not feeling himself bound by literary or philological conventions. Then it is important to remember that Mark did not know that the later generations would suppose that that was how a gospel ought to end. On the contrary, he may have realized that the Resurrection was indescribable and so left his readers in awe and wonder before the empty tomb. From a literary point of view the present ending may seem to be a monstrosity but from a theological point of view it may be a stroke of genius. Mark's gospel begins abruptly: 'In divinity', said Bacon, 'many things must be left abrupt.' Some words of Robert Leighton are also to the point: 'There is no speaking of it; a curtain is drawn; silent wonder expresses it best – telling you that it cannot be expressed.'

Present-day readers must decide for themselves which of these two views of the ending of the gospel is the more convincing. See also note on v. 8 below.

16:1 And when the sabbath was past, Mary Magdalene, and Mary the mother of James, and Salome, bought spices, so that they might go and anoint him. 2 And very early on the first day of the week they went to the tomb when the sun had risen. 3 And they were saying to one another, 'Who will roll away the stone for us from the door of the tomb?' 4 And looking up, they saw that the stone was rolled back – it was very large. 5 And entering the tomb, they saw a young man sitting on the right side, dressed in a white robe; and they were amazed. 6 And he said to them, 'Do not be amazed; you seek Jesus of Nazareth, who was crucified. He has risen, he is not here; see the place where they laid him. 7 But go, tell his disciples and Peter that he is going before you to Galilee; there you will see him, as he told you.' 8 And they went out and fled from the tomb; for trembling and astonishment had come upon them; and they said nothing to any one, for they were afraid.

16:1 *When the sabbath was past* i.e. on Saturday evening they bought spices for use on Sunday morning. *Mary Magdalene and . . .* The fact that women play so prominent a part in the records about the first Easter morning is evidence for their authenticity, since the early Church would not have made up such stories in view of the Jewish attitude to women. It is true that there are irreconcilable discrepancies in the gospel records, but so there are in many eyewitness accounts of contemporary happenings. *So that they might go and anoint him* It was the custom in Palestine for relatives and friends to visit the grave of a dead person fo. three days after burial.

16:2 *Very early on the first day of the week* This would seem to indicate about 4 a.m., though this is inconsistent with the following words *when the sun had risen*. Henry met the difficulty thus: 'Either they had a long walk, or met with some hindrance, so that it was sun-rising by the time they got to the sepulchre.'

16:4 *It was very large* One would have expected these words to have come at the end of v. 3 and some manuscripts did transpose them there.

16:5 *A young man . . . in a white robe* He is certainly intended to be an angel, though some have vainly imagined that he was the young man of 14:51f. 'It is probable that Mark's description is imaginative; he picturesquely describes what he believes happened' (T). 'I believe and understand the ministrations of holy angels, as clarkes tell; but it was not shewed me; for himself is nearest and meekest, highest and lowest, and doth all' (Mother Julian).

16:6 *He has risen* – one word in Greek and a passive verb. The New Testament normally refers to the Resurrection as an act of God.

16:7 *Go, tell his disciples and Peter* 'Had the angel said

only, *Go tell the disciples*, poor Peter would have been ready to sigh, and say, But I doubt I cannot look upon myself as one of them, for I disowned him, and deserve to be disowned by him' (H). *He is going before you to Galilee* See note on 14:28.

16:8 *Trembling and astonishment had come upon them; and they said nothing to any one, for they were afraid* Fear and amazement are the normal responses in the Bible to divine revelations. 'The women's awe mirrors the incomprehensible, powerful, overwhelming message: Jesus the crucified has risen' (Sch). 'The resurrection of Jesus is as an event the utterly incomprehensible and transcendent, the beginning of the *Parousia*' (Emil Brunner).

The late Professor R. H. Lightfoot, who was one of the most sensitive interpreters of Mark's gospel, deploring that 'the awe or dread or holy fear of God' had largely disappeared in the religious life of Christendom, wrote: 'If the belief should ever come to be widely held that St Mark may have ended his book deliberately at 16:8, I should like to think that such a recognition might have its part to play in recalling men and women to the truth that the dread as well as the love of God is an essential note of our religion, which sounds loudly in the New Testament as well as in the Old, and in no book of the New Testament more strongly than in the Gospel according to St Mark.'

Abbreviations

A.V.	The Authorized, or King James, Version of the Bible
Ba	*William Barclay*, The New Testament: a new translation (Collins)
Be	*J. A. Bengel*, Gnomon of the New Testament
Br	*B. H. Branscomb*, The Gospel of Mark (Moffatt Commentary)
C	*John Calvin*, Commentary on a Harmony of the Evangelists
Ca	*Philip Carrington*, According to Mark
Cr	*C. E. B. Cranfield*, The Gospel according to St Mark (Cambridge Greek Testament Commentary) (C.U.P.)
Go	*E. J. Goodspeed*, The New Testament: an American translation (University of Chicago Press)
Gr	*F. C. Grant*, The Gospel according to St Mark (Interpreter's Bible)
H	*Matthew Henry*, An Exposition of the New Testament
Hu	*A. M. Hunter*, The Gospel according to St Mark (Torch Commentaries) (SCM Press)
Jo	**S. E. Johnson*, The Gospel According to St Mark (A. & C. Black)
J	The Jerusalem Bible (Darton, Longman & Todd)
K	*R. A. Knox*, The New Testament in English (Burns, Oates)
Li	*R. H. Lightfoot*, The Gospel Message of St Mark
Lo	*A. Loisy*, L'Evangile selon Marc
LXX	The Septuagint or Greek Version of the Old Testament
M	*James Moffatt*, The New Testament: a new translation (Hodder & Stoughton)

N	*D. E. Nineham*, The Gospel of St Mark (Pelican Commentary)
N.E.B.	The New English Bible
N.T.	New Testament
O.T.	Old Testament
P	*J. B. Phillips*, The New Testament in Modern English (Collins)
R	*A. E. J. Rawlinson*, The Gospel according to St Mark (Westminster Commentary)
R.S.V.	Revised Standard Version, or The Common Bible
R.V.	The Revised Version of the Bible
Sc	*Thomas Scott*, The New Testament with explanatory notes
Sch	*Rudolf Schnackenburg*, The Gospel according to St Mark (Sheed and Ward)
Sw	*H. B. Swete*, The Gospel according to St Mark (Macmillan)
T	*Vincent Taylor*, The Gospel according to St Mark (Macmillan)
We	*R. F. Weymouth*, New Testament in modern speech (J. Clarke)
Wi	*C. B. Williams*, The New Testament: a private translation

* Recommended for further and more detailed study

Books listed against individual authors' names and for which there is no publisher shown are not at present in print, so far as is known.